InstaEnglish

Student's Book and Workbook

2nd Edition

2B

Emma Heyderman
Fiona Mauchline
Patrick Howarth
Patricia Reilly
Olivia Johnston

macmillan education

InstaEnglish
Student's Book and Workbook
2nd Edition
WALKTHROUGH

Check out how your combo edition of the **Student's Book and Workbook** is structured so you can make the most of it!

STUDENT'S BOOK

Your **Student's Book** is made up of a **Starter unit**, **8 regular units**, 4 sets of **review activities**, plus 2 nifty sections: **Digital Literacy** after every 2 units, and **Global Citizenship** after every 4 units.

Starter unit

This two-page unit provides strategic language for you to kick off your studies!

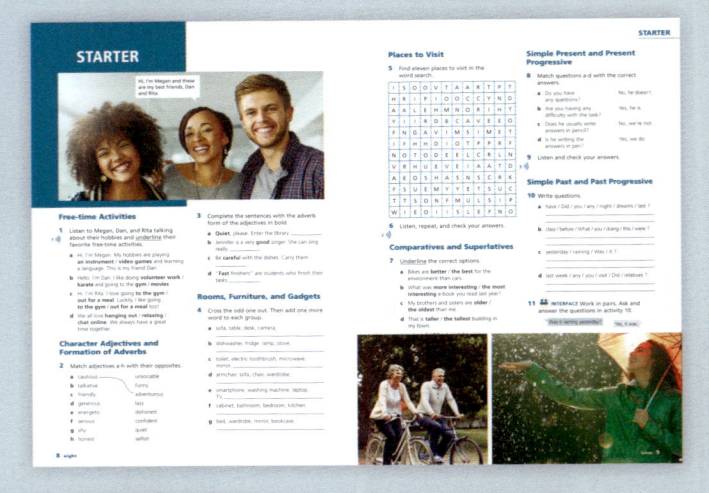

Opener

All regular units open with a visual treat to trigger your first thoughts on the main subject. What's the first thing that pops into your head when you look at it?

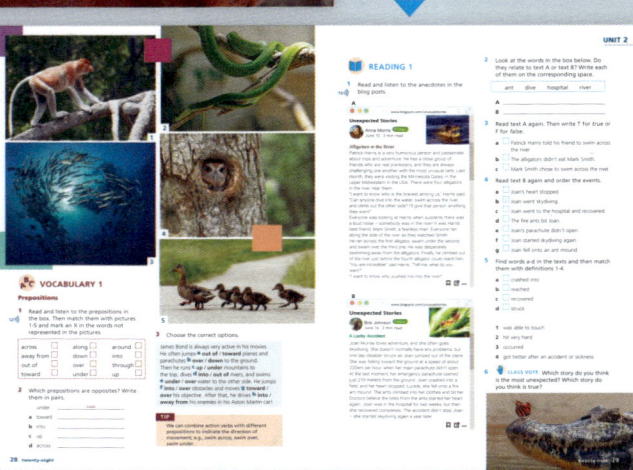

2 UNEXPECTED BUT TRUE

READING 1

Texts of multiple genres provide interesting content to practice your reading skills and introduce relevant language to be explored throughout the unit.

VOCABULARY 1

Here you will read, listen to, and look at pictures referring to words or phrases that will help you to explore the unit topic.

2 two

🔑 GRAMMAR 1
Grammar topics that were introduced in the reading text are systematically explored so you can easily work out all the rules and patterns.

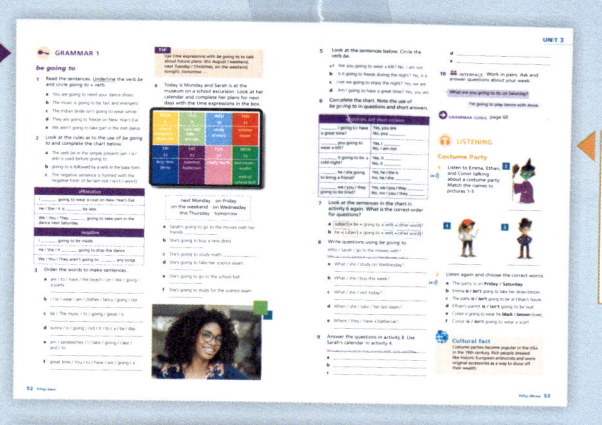

🎧 LISTENING
Learn and practice oral comprehension through engaging and contextualized oral texts.

💬 SPEAKING
A clearly guided activity will help you practice your speaking skills using functional language in everyday situations. Throughout the levels, as you improve your ability to communicate orally, you will get increasing contact with real-life oral text genres.

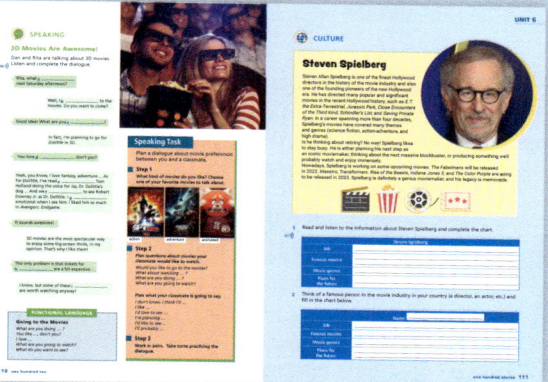

🌐 CULTURE
Discover cultural aspects of everyday life in English-speaking countries across the globe!

🔤 VOCABULARY 2
The second vocabulary set provides more words and phrases to allow you to go further into the unit topic.

📖 READING 2
The second reading text digs further into the main topic and provides more language to be explored.

🔑 GRAMMAR 2
A new grammar topic is introduced in the same contextualized and systematic way seen in **Grammar 1**.

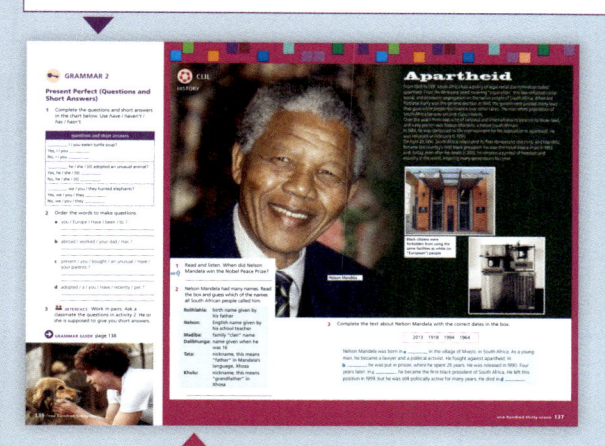

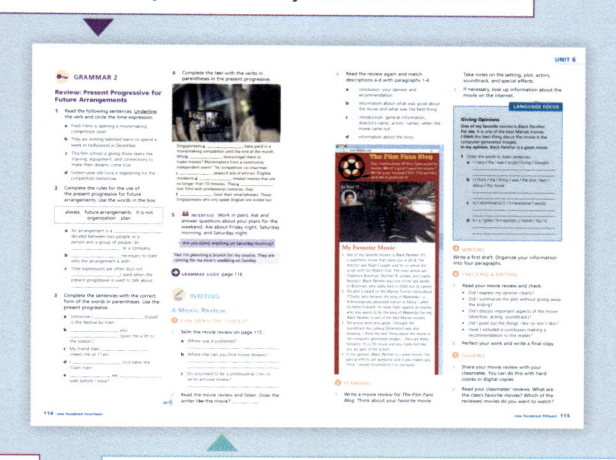

⚙️ CLIL
In every odd-numbered unit, the **Grammar 2** section is accompanied by the **CLIL** section, for you to integrate your learning of the English language with other school subjects through fun texts and activities.

✏️ WRITING
In even-numbered units, the **Grammar 2** section is followed by the **Writing** section, where you are supported every step of the way to practice your writing skills in a range of text genres.

three **3**

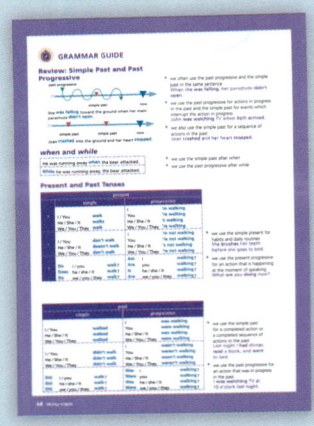

GRAMMAR GUIDE
This is a reference section for all the grammar topics explored in the unit.

VOCABULARY IN PICTURES
Have fun reviewing all the words and phrases learned in the **Vocabulary** sections, all richly illustrated!

PROGRESS CHECK
Once you complete the unit, cut this page out and close your book. Do the activities and check your overall progress. Then go back to the **Grammar Guide** and the **Vocabulary in Pictures** pages and revise anything you missed.

Review
Review the vocabulary and grammar from the previous two units starting with a game!

DIGITAL LITERACY
Do you think you use digital technology wisely? Follow siblings Lily and Daniel in a manga-style comic and see how they interact *with* and *through* the digital universe while reflecting about their (and your) relationship with the "digital."

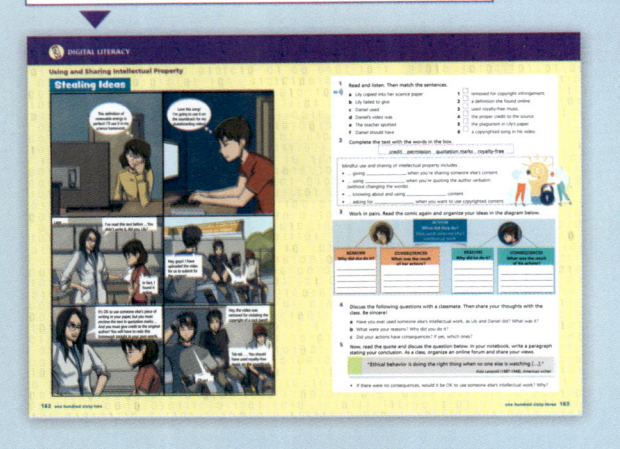

GLOBAL CITIZENSHIP
All of us need to nurture the perception that we are part of the same world. We need to build knowledge and develop skills to live together in the best possible way. That's what this section is all about!

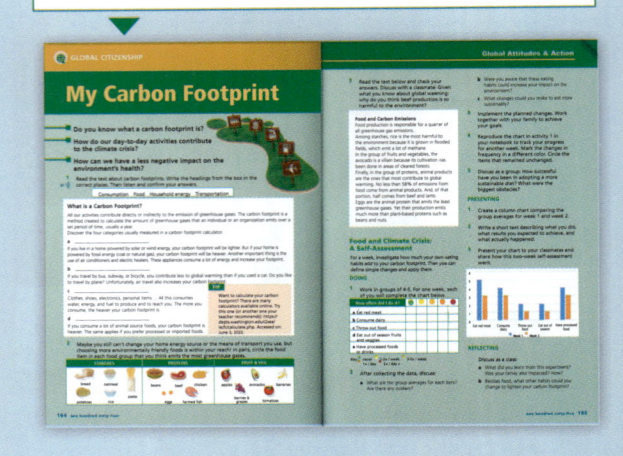

The **TIP, READING STRATEGY, PRONUNCIATION, CULTURAL FACT, FUNCTIONAL LANGUAGE, LANGUAGE FOCUS, CLASS VOTE,** and **INTERFACE** features will make your learning process more practical and effective.

WORKBOOK

The **Workbook** offers target-language practice and additional study material (consolidation and extension). It can be used as homework, independent study, or extra classroom practice. Some of the sections correspond to sections in the **Student's Book**:

VOCABULARY 1

GRAMMAR 1

VOCABULARY 2

GRAMMAR 2

GRAMMAR CHECK
A text with interesting and curious facts helps you check your reading and language skills.

LISTENING

EXTENSION
This engaging section offers an extra challenge on grammar and vocabulary items.

VOCABULARY PLUS
Learn more words related to the unit topic in a fun way! All words are illustrated.

Wordlist

This offers an alphabetical list of the key vocabulary in the **Student's Book** and from the **Vocabulary Plus** sections. It includes phonetic transcriptions and audio recordings.

DIGITAL OFFERINGS

InstaEnglish **2nd Edition** is a fully flexible course, which means you can study using your physical or your digital books and have access to the exact same content and activities. The digital books contain all the audio tracks and videos embedded. The digital offerings include the **On-the-go Practice** feature, for you to keep learning wherever you are!

CONTENTS

UNIT	VOCABULARY	GRAMMAR	READING
5 AMBITIONS 88	1 Life Events 90 2 Musical Instruments 96	1 will / won't 92 2 First Conditional 98	1 Know Your Future 91 2 Mr. Music Answers 96
6 ON SCREEN 104	1 Movies 106 2 Suffixes -ion and -ment 112	1 Future Form: will; Future Form: be going to 108 2 Review: Present Progressive for Future Arrangements 114	1 Trends in Moviemaking 107 2 Make a Movie in Hollywood! 113

REVIEW 3 120

UNIT	VOCABULARY	GRAMMAR	READING
7 THE WORLD WE LIVE IN 126	1 Materials and Containers 128 2 Endangered Animals 134	1 Present Perfect (Affirmative and Negative) 130 2 Present Perfect (Questions and Short Answers) 136	1 It's Your World! 129 2 Adopt an Animal! 134
8 ALTRUISM 142	1 Fundraising Ideas 144 2 make and do 150	1 Present Perfect: ever, never, yet, already, just 146 2 Present Perfect: for and since 152	1 A Newspaper Article 145 2 Selena Gomez, Goodwill Ambassador 150

REVIEW 4 158

GLOBAL CITIZENSHIP – MY CARBON FOOTPRINT 164

IRREGULAR VERBS 166

WORKBOOK 167

WORDLIST 234

LISTENING	SPEAKING	CULTURE	CLIL	WRITING
Ambitions 93	An Interview on Future Plans 94	Three Great Career Fields in the USA 95	ICT: Dot-com Companies 99	
3D Movies 109	3D Movies Are Awesome! 110	Steven Spielberg 111		A Movie Review 114

DIGITAL LITERACY – HOW TO SELECT SOURCES OF INFORMATION 124

Eco Family 131	A Fundraising Bike Ride 132	New Zealand Loves Cycling 133	History: Apartheid 136	
Charity Appeals 147	An Audio Ad about a Fundraising Event 148	Good Deeds Day in India 149		A Newsletter Article 152

DIGITAL LITERACY – USING AND SHARING INTELLECTUAL PROPERTY 162

5

AMBITIONS

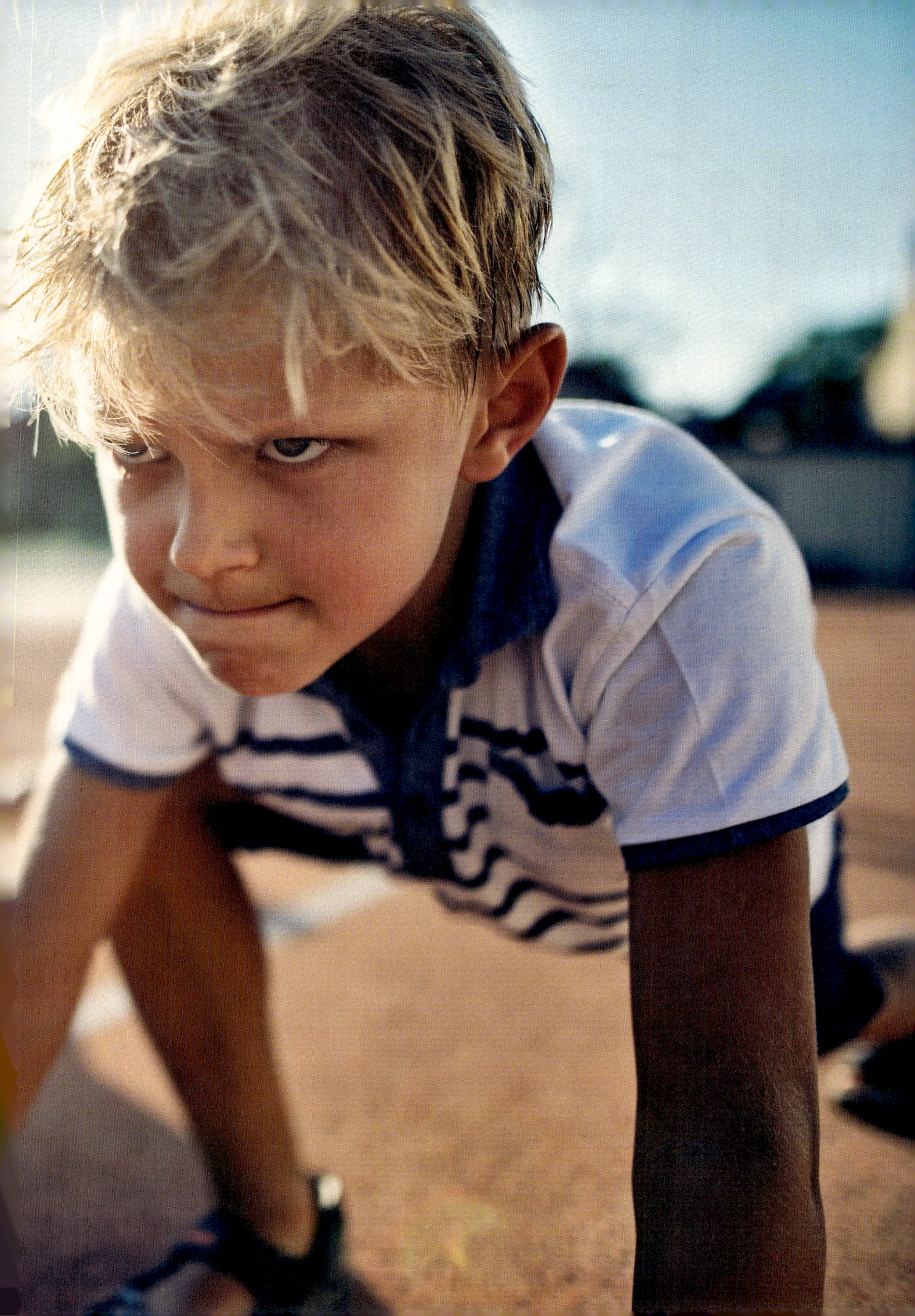

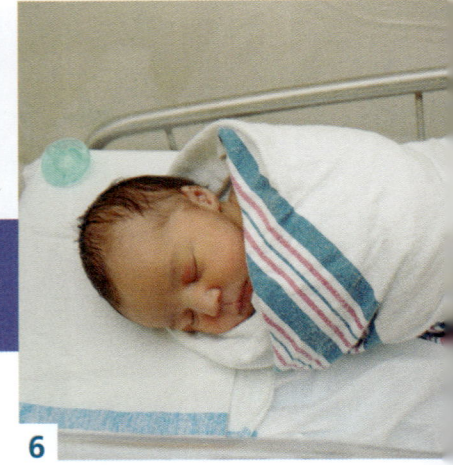

VOCABULARY 1

Life Events

1 Which of the words in the box describe the events in the pictures?

be born ☐	learn to drive ☐
buy a house ☐	leave home ☐
get a job ☐	leave school ☐
get married ☐	start school ☐
go to college ☐	train to be a … ☐
have children ☐	work ☐

2 Listen and repeat.

🔊 42

3 Complete the sentences with the correct form of the words in activity 1.

a I want to _____ to study chemistry when I am 18.

b I _____ to John last September.

c I _____ when I was 5 years old.

d In the USA, you can _____ a car when you're 16.

e My dad _____ in a hospital in Minneapolis in 1962.

f My aunt _____ two _____. Their names are Sara and Tarik.

> **TIP**
>
> The word *ambition* is used to talk about plans, aspirations, and desires, and not only about things that we really want and are difficult to achieve.

4 Based on the sentences in activity 3, write about your story and your plans.

_____
_____
_____
_____
_____

90 ninety

UNIT 5

📖 READING 1

1 Read the sentences. Then write T for *true* or F for *false*.

a ☐ British boys leave home later than girls.
b ☐ People get married younger in Spain than in Portugal.
c ☐ The Chinese have more children than the Americans.
d ☐ The Swedes live longer than the Americans.

2 Read the statistics, listen, and check your answers.

🔊 43

Know Your Future

Don't read your horoscope, but instead look at the demographics for your country if you want to know your future. Demographics can tell you, for example, that, if you are born in Japan, you'll probably have one child and live until you are 83. They are statistics about real people in real places, and they can be fun. Here are some more …

Leaving Home
If you're a Finnish girl, you'll probably leave home when you're about 21. The average Finnish boy won't leave home until he's nearly 23. In Spain and Portugal, a girl will leave home at about 27, but a boy won't leave home until he's nearly 30. In the UK, the average girl will leave home at 23 and a boy, at 25.

Getting Married
A person born in Bolivia, Portugal, or the USA will get married for the first time at about 23 or 24 years old. In the UK, Spain, or Japan, it'll happen at 29. If you want to wait, go to Finland, France, or Germany – they get married at 30.

Having Children
In the USA, you'll probably have two children. But the math is more complicated in other countries. In the UK and China, a family will have 1.8 children, but in Spain they'll have 1.4 – the same as in Portugal. Do you want more? Go to Bolivia, where the average family has 3.4 children.

Age
How long will you live? Iceland is a good place to live as you'll probably live to around 82. This is similar to Sweden (81) and better than the USA (78), Turkey (72), or Russia (67).

3 Scan the text and answer the questions.

a What do demographics tell you about living in Japan?
_____
b How old are Finnish girls when they leave home?
_____
c Where do people get married at 30?
_____
d How many children does the average American have?
_____
e Which country has the most children per family?
_____
f According to the text, is Sweden a good place to live? Why?
_____

READING STRATEGY

There are many words that end in *-ics* in English. Noticing some suffix patterns can help you predict meanings and better understand some texts. For example, do you think the words *demographics*, *statistics*, and *mathematics* are nouns, adjectives, or adverbs?

4 Look at the words in the box. How do you say them in your language?

> aerobics   computer graphics
> economics   physics   politics

5 ✋ **CLASS VOTE** Look at the demographics in the text. Which country would you like to live in?

ninety-one **91**

🔑 GRAMMAR 1

will / won't

1 Read the following sentences. Underline the verbs in the affirmative form and circle those in the negative form.

   a In Finland, the average girl will leave home at 21.
   b The average British boy won't leave home until he's 25.
   c In the USA, you'll probably have two children.
   d In China, people won't have many children.

2 Use the words in the box to complete the chart.

> 'll   will (×2)   won't (×2)

affirmative	negative
I / You _____ get married soon.	I / You _____ have children.
He / She / It _____ live to around 84.	He / She / It will not get married.
We / You / They _____ leave home at an older age.	We / You / They _____ live long.

3 Look at the sentences in the chart and check (✓) the rules for the use of will / won't.

   a ☐ will / won't are used to express past ideas.
   b ☐ will / won't are followed by the base form of the main verb.
   c ☐ The short form of will is 'll and the short form of will not is won't.

4 Write complete sentences. Use will (✓) and won't (✗).

   a I / learn to drive / at 17. (✗)
   _____

   b He / leave home / at 18. (✓)
   _____

   c They / have two children. (✗)
   _____

   d We / buy / a small house. (✓)
   _____

5 Complete the post with will and won't and the verbs in the box.

> be   get (not)   go   leave
> study   train   travel

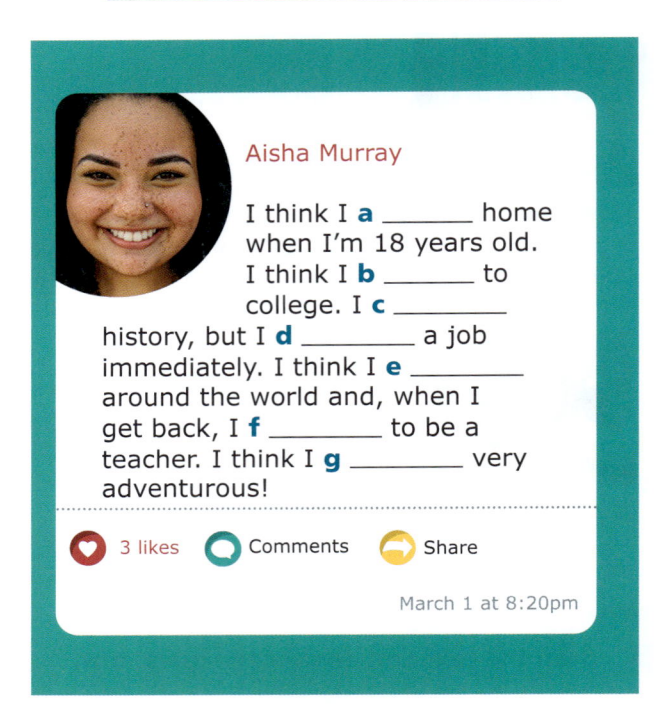

Aisha Murray

I think I **a** _____ home when I'm 18 years old. I think I **b** _____ to college. I **c** _____ history, but I **d** _____ a job immediately. I think I **e** _____ around the world and, when I get back, I **f** _____ to be a teacher. I think I **g** _____ very adventurous!

❤ 3 likes   💬 Comments   ↗ Share

March 1 at 8:20pm

TIP

When we make predictions, we often use time expressions like *soon*, *tomorrow*, and *next month*. We also use phrases with *when*: *I'll work in education when I'm older.*

6 Complete the sentences so they are true for you.

   a I hope we'll _____ tomorrow.
   b I won't _____ when I'm 16.
   c I think I'll _____ next summer.
   d We'll _____ one day soon.
   e We won't _____ this weekend.

UNIT 5

7 Read the information below and complete the chart.

   a Use *will* before the subject in questions.

   b For short answers, use *will* in the affirmative form and *won't* in the negative form.

questions and short answers
_____ I / you leave home at 24?
Yes, I / you _____.   No, I / you _____.
_____ he / she / it be here soon?
Yes, he / she / it _____.
No, he / she / it _____.
_____ we / you / they get married next month?
Yes, we / you / they _____.
No, we / you / they _____.

8 Write complete questions. Use *will*.

your family / always / live / in the same house?
Will your family always live in the same house?

   a you / study / to be a vet / at college?
   _____

   b you / have / good job / one day?
   _____

   c your friend / play basketball / tomorrow?
   _____

   d everybody / buy / cars?
   _____

PRONUNCIATION

will ('ll)

1 Listen to the sentences. Do you hear 1 or 2?

44 🔊   **a** **1** I go to college.   **2** I'll go to college.

            b **1** I have two children.   **2** I'll have two children.

   2 Listen again and repeat.

44 🔊

9 👥 **INTERFACE** Work in pairs. Make predictions about your future using the ideas in the box.

| drive a vintage car   get married |
| go to college   travel the world |

> What will you do?

> I think I'll go to college.

➡ **GRAMMAR GUIDE** page 100

🎧 LISTENING

Ambitions

1 Grace and Benjamin are 13 years old and they're talking about their future. Listen and complete their ambitions with a phrase in the box.

45 🔊

| big car   dentist   DJ |
| get married at 21   India   the world |

Grace

   a I'll work as a _____.

   b I think I'll work in _____.

   c One day I'll travel _____.

Benjamin

   d I'll be a _____.

   e I'll buy a _____.

   f I'll _____.

2 Listen to Grace and Benjamin aged 29. How many of their ambitions came true?

46 🔊

_____
_____
_____
_____

3 Listen again and answer the questions.

46 🔊

   a What did Grace study at college?
   _____

   b Which country does Grace frequently travel to?
   _____

   c What is Benjamin's job?
   _____

   d How many children does Benjamin have?
   _____

SPEAKING

An Interview on Future Plans

1 Maggie is interviewing teenagers for her podcast. Read and listen. What is the main interview question?

🔊 47

_____
_____

INTERVIEW 1

Maggie: Hi! Can you do a quick interview for my podcast?
Adam: Yes, sure.
Maggie: Thanks! So could you tell me your name and how old you are?
Adam: My name's Adam and I'm 14 years old.
Maggie: Okay. Tell me, Adam, what do you want to do when you finish high school?
Adam: Well, that'll be five years from now … If I don't change my mind, I'll take a gap year.
Maggie: A gap year? What for?
Adam: Well, I think it will be an excellent way to grow personally. If I take a gap year, I'll volunteer abroad. It'll be a great opportunity to learn about the real world and to contribute to a community in need.
Maggie: That sounds great, Adam. Thanks for the interview!
Adam: You're welcome.

INTERVIEW 2

Maggie: Hello! Can you do a quick interview for my podcast?
Amelia: No problem.
Maggie: Great! So could you tell me your name and how old you are?
Amelia: My name's Amelia and I'm 13 years old.
Maggie: Okay. Tell me, Amelia, what do you want to do when you finish high school?
Amelia: Well, I want to be at college five years from now. I think I'll study law.
Maggie: Right here in Madison?
Amelia: No … I'll probably live in another city, have some independence.
Maggie: You have big plans, Amelia! Congratulations … and thanks for the interview.
Amelia: You're welcome. Take care!

2 Read the interviews again.

  a What questions were planned? <u>Underline</u> them.

  b What are follow-up questions? Circle them.

> **TIP**
> In an interview, the interviewer usually plans a list of questions. Then they might ask follow-up questions depending on how the interviewee answers the previous question.

FUNCTIONAL LANGUAGE

Talking about the Future
What do you want to do when you finish high school?
Five years from now, I'll …
I want to …
I think I'll …
I'll probably …

Speaking Task

Take turns interviewing and being interviewed by a classmate about future plans.

Step 1

First, think about things you want to do in five or six years' time.

Step 2

Think about what you will say when you are interviewed.
Five years from now, I'll … / I want to …
I think I'll …
I'll probably …

Plan the questions you will ask as an interviewer.
Can you do a quick interview for my podcast?
Please tell me what your name is and how old you are.
What do you want to do when you finish high school?

Also think about some follow-up questions.
What do you want to major in?
Do you plan to work?
What are you planning to take this gap year for?

Step 3

Find a quiet place and record the interviews with a cell phone.
Using a cloud storage service, upload class interviews.
Listen to your classmates' interviews and discuss as a class:
What are the most common plans among your classmates?
Does anyone want to study abroad? In which country?
Is anyone planning to take a gap year? What for?

UNIT 5

🌐 CULTURE

Three Great Career Fields in the USA

Lots of people face disappointment when job hunting. There is a lot of competition and little job growth in many fields. Taking that into consideration, what jobs can young Americans look for in the years to come?
That question can be difficult to answer. You need to consider the best potential for job growth, pay, stress level, job satisfaction, among other factors. Three of the most prominent fields are:

Medical Field:
In this area, nurses are in demand. Nurse practitioners can perform some of the functions of a doctor, such as prescribing medicine and treating diseases. Physician assistants are also climbing in America. They conduct physical exams, prescribe medicine, and treat diseases. And their pay is quite high!

Technology Sector:
This is a fast-growing field. Information technology is the #1 field in terms of expected job growth over the next decade, which makes systems engineers among the most in-demand professionals today.

Financial Services:
Many American companies are putting an end to their pension plans and employees will need help with retirement planning. Therefore, jobs in accounting are expected to grow over the next decade.
As technology and business evolve quickly, new careers will come and go just as fast. So Americans understand how important it is to choose a career field that will be in high demand for the future ahead.

---

1 Read and listen. Then match.

🔊 48

a Americans will take into consideration the best potential for job growth, pay, stress level, and job satisfaction …
b Nursing careers will be in demand …
c The #1 field in terms of expected growth …
d Accounting will be on the rise …

☐ … because employees will need help with retirement planning.
☐ … because of the need for professionals in the area who can prescribe medicine and treat diseases.
☐ … when looking for a job in the future.
☐ … is the technology sector.

2 Which careers are on the rise in your country? Talk to some experts / family members about it.
_____
_____

3 Which of these areas interests you? Why? Share your ideas with your classmates.
_____
_____

VOCABULARY 2

Musical Instruments

1 Match the words in the box to the pictures.

> acoustic guitar ☐   drums ☐   electric bass ☐   electric guitar ☐
> flute ☐   keyboard ☐   percussion ☐   piano ☐
> saxophone ☐   trumpet ☐   violin ☐

2 Listen and repeat.

🔊 49

3 Look at the picture and complete the sentences with words from activity 1.

a   Josh plays _____.
b   Marc plays _____.
c   Lars plays _____.
d   Anne plays _____.

READING 2

1 Skim the texts on the next page. What genre do they illustrate?

a   A magazine article.
b   An advice column.

2 Read and listen to the texts. Then complete with the challenge each reader faces.

🔊 50

a   Bandless Musician wants _____.
b   Poor Violinist wants _____.

Mr. Music Answers

> I really want to be in a band, but I have no idea where to start. Many friends have their own bands and I feel embarrassed to ask them. What should I do?

Bandless Musician

Dear Bandless Musician, if you want to be in a successful band, you'll need at least one singer and three friends to play the guitar, the drums, and the keyboard or electric bass. It's important to practice every day. If you don't practice, you'll sound terrible and people won't like your music or buy your songs.

Your look is important too. If you want to be famous, you'll need an image to make you different. If people don't recognize your image as well as your music, they won't remember you immediately. If you have a unique image, your fans will love you. They'll buy your songs, they'll go to your concerts and ... congratulations! You will be the next big thing!

> I started playing the violin in a charity project in my town. But when the project ended, I had to stop practicing. My family cannot afford a violin, which is a very expensive instrument. I really want to play again! What should I do?

Poor Violinist

Dear Poor Violinist, if you look through the classified ads, you'll find second-hand violins at a good price. You can also apply for a scholarship to a music school. Many schools offer scholarships to talented students from lower income. If you get a scholarship, you'll improve your skills with qualified instructors.

Finally, one last idea is to seek sponsorship. If a company in your city sees talent in you, it will help you financially. In return, you will advertise for it. Research some potential sponsors and email them explaining your situation. Good luck!

---

3 Read the texts again and answer the questions.

a What is the minimum number of people in a successful band?

b If you want to play in a band, how often should you practice your songs?

c What can make you different from other bands?

d Where can you find cheap violins?

e Who do music schools usually give scholarships to?

f What does a sponsor expect from a musician in return for their financial help?

TIP

Like words ending in *-ics*, words ending in *-ship* are nouns. In general, the suffix *-ship* is added to another noun. For example, a *sponsor* provides a *sponsorship*, *friends* have *friendship*.
Taking that into account, what do you think the nouns below mean?
dictatorship   kingship
ownership   partnership

4 Work in pairs. Write one more piece of advice for each of the readers.

a For Bandless Musician

b For Poor Violinist

GRAMMAR 2

First Conditional

1 Read the sentences below. <u>Underline</u> the *if clause* and circle the *consequence*.

  a If you want to be a successful band, you'll need at least one singer.
  b If you don't practice, you'll sound terrible.
  c You'll need an image to make you different if you want to become famous.
  d Your fans will love you if you have a unique image.

2 Look at the sentences in activity 1. Choose the correct options to complete the rules for the use of the first conditional.

  a We form the first conditional with *if* + **simple past** / **simple present**, *will* / *won't* + main verb in the base form.
  b We use the first conditional to talk about possibilities in the **past** / **future**.
  c Use a comma when the *if* clause is at **the beginning of the sentence** / **the end of the sentence**.

3 Now complete the charts with the words provided.

| don't like | 'll be | sings | won't sell |

if clause	consequence
If people _____ your image,	they won't buy your songs.
If you practice,	you'_____ a good singer.

consequence	*if* clause
You _____ anything	if you aren't a good singer.
The singer will become famous	if he _____ well.

4 Match the two parts to make sentences.

  a If you study music every day,
  b I will buy their new album
  c If I don't have enough money for a guitar,
  d We'll all cry tears of joy
  e You won't learn any new songs
  f If I say that dinner's ready,

☐ if he wins the singing contest.
☐ if you don't practice.
☐ you'll learn to play an instrument.
☐ he'll stop playing his guitar.
☐ if I have enough money.
☐ I will borrow one.

5 Write complete sentences.

If I learn German, I / be able to / work / in Switzerland.
<u>If I learn German, I'll be able to work in Switzerland.</u>

  a He'll borrow a minibus if / he / want / to travel across the USA.
  _____
  b If you practice regularly, you / play / really well.
  _____
  c If a group has a strong image, some of their fans / probably / copy it.
  _____
  d If you share it with friends, you / enjoy / the music more.
  _____

6 Complete the sentences with the correct form of the verbs in parentheses.

  a If you _____ (come) to my house later, my dad _____ (cook) us pasta.
  b If I _____ (not clean up) my room, my mom _____ (not buy) that new computer game.
  c He _____ (not be) able to play basketball if he _____ (arrive) late.
  d If she _____ (not arrive) before 9pm, we _____ (go) to the concert without her.

7 Complete the sentences using your own ideas.

  a If it rains on the weekend, _____
  b If I go to college, _____
  c I will visit my friends if _____

8 **INTERFACE** Work in pairs. Compare your answers to activity 7.

> What will you do if it rains on the weekend?

> If it rains on the weekend, I'll stay home reading *The Lord of the Rings*.

➡ **GRAMMAR GUIDE** page 100

CLIL

ICT

1 Read and listen. What do you think a dot-com company is?

Dot-com Companies

Silicon Valley is in southern of San Francisco, California. It's home to many large technology companies such as Apple and Hewlett-Packard, and also many dot-com companies. These are companies like Google, Facebook, and eBay, which operate mainly over the internet.

But where did the dot-com company come from?

In 1985, the World Wide Web was first introduced to the world. A company called Symbolics became the first company to register its address, or URL, on the web. Today, there are 200 million websites in existence, and one domain is registered every three minutes in the UK alone. But it took a long time for the internet to become the phenomenon it is today. It was when Sir Tim Berners-Lee put up the first website in 1990 (info.cern.ch) that the internet took off.

During the 1990s, there was a dot-com boom. Many people became rich because of the World Wide Web. In 1998, PhD students Larry Page and Sergey Brin invented Google. These days, this search engine is the world's most recognizable brand and, in 2022, the company is worth nearly $2 trillion.

2 Find four dot-com companies in the word search.

O	E	O	G	D	G	L	A
Y	W	W	L	O	O	F	P
F	A	C	E	B	O	O	K
A	P	S	U	M	G	F	L
C	P	G	A	P	L	L	F
E	L	O	O	G	E	B	A
R	E	R	E	B	A	Y	C

3 Choose the correct answers.

   a What does "www" mean?
      1 World Wide Web
      2 World World Website
      3 We Work WorldWide

   b What is a URL?
      1 a computer virus
      2 a web page address
      3 an email address

   c Which of these is not an internet browser?
      1 Internet Explorer
      2 Google Chrome
      3 Amazon

   d What "language" do you use to create a web page?
      1 HTML   **2** URL   **3** HTTP

GRAMMAR GUIDE

will / won't

affirmative	
I / You / He / She / It / We / You / They	will have

negative	
I / You / He / She / It / We / You / They	will not (won't) have

- we use *will / won't* + the main verb in the base form to make predictions
  I **will** have a lot of children.
  She **won't** live in Australia.
- we often use the expressions *I think*, *I expect*, *I guess* to introduce predictions
  He **thinks** he**'ll be** famous.
  I **expect** they**'ll get** married.
- *can* is never used with *will / won't*. To talk about ability in the future, use *will / won't* + *be able to*
  He**'ll be able to** learn French in Canada.
- we often use these time expressions with *will*: *one day*, *one day soon*, *soon*, *tomorrow*, *next year*, *when I'm older*, *when I finish school*
  I**'ll buy a car when I'm 20**.
  He**'ll go to college next year**.

questions and short answers
Will I / you / he / she / it / we / you / they **go**?
Yes, they **will**.   No, they **won't**.

- the word order is different in questions
  He **will** be a famous football player.
  Will he be a famous football player?
- we don't repeat the infinitive in short answers
  Will we buy a big house?
  Yes, we **will**.

First Conditional

situation	consequence
If I **eat** all the food,	I**'ll** feel sick.
If she **passes** the exam,	she**'ll** go to college.

consequence	situation
He **won't** eat popcorn	**if** he **goes** to the movies.
They **will** be happy	**if** they **pass** the driver's test.

- we use the first conditional to talk about possible situations and their consequences
- to form first conditional sentences we use
  if + subject + present simple (for the situation), subject + *will / won't* + the main verb in the base form (for the consequence)
- if the situation comes first, we need a comma
  If you practice, you'll get better.
- we don't use a comma if the consequence comes first
  I will be happy **if I pass** my exams.

PROGRESS CHECK

Name: _____
Class name / Period: _____
Teacher: _____
Date: _____

Life Events

1 Identify the life events.

1. b __ b __ __ __
2. s __ __ __ __
   s __ __ __ __
3. g __ __
   m __ __ r i __ __
4. g __ __ a j __ __
5. l __ __ __ __
   t __ d __ __ __ e
6. l __ __ __ __
   h __ __ __

Musical Instruments

2 Order the letters to write musical instruments.

a oxophsaen   _____
b mudrs   _____
c tufle   _____
d nliivo   _____
e spsrcneuoi   _____
f cusaitco tgiura   _____
g tpmtreu   _____
h ybrkedoa   _____

will / won't

3 Complete the sentences with *will / won't*.

In 2030 …

a more people _____ (be) older than 65.
b I _____ (have) a good job.
c we _____ (use) only computers to study.
d more people _____ (not get) married.
e I _____ (not drive) a car, but I _____ (ride) a bike to work.
f The population of the world _____ (be) 9 billion.

4 Order the words to make questions.

a you / when you're older / Will / live abroad ?
_____
_____

b go to college / when you are 18 / you / Will ?
_____
_____

c you / one day / train / Will / to be a doctor ?
_____
_____

First Conditional

5 Write complete sentences.

a If / he / want / to be an actor / he / go / to drama school.
_____
_____

b If / he / go / to drama school / they / teach him to speak clearly.
_____
_____
_____

c He / live / in Hollywood / if / he / become / a successful actor.
_____
_____

Grammar Buildup 5

1 2 3 4 5 **6** 7 8

6   Complete the dialogue. Use the correct form of the verbs in parentheses.

Dad   What **a** _____ you _____ (look) at?

Lizie   I **b** _____ (think) about my future and I **c** _____ (not be) sure what subjects to choose.

Dad   Oh! What **d** _____ (be) the options?

Lizie   I **e** _____ (look) at the options right now. All my friends **f** _____ (go) to do biology and chemistry.

Dad   Well, what do you want to do in the future?

Lizie   That's the problem. I **g** _____ (want) to work with animals two years ago. Now I think I **h** _____ (work) with people.

Dad   If you **i** _____ (write) a list of your favorite subjects, you **j** _____ (know) which subjects to do.

Lizie   Thanks a lot, dad. That's a really good idea.

UNIT 5

VOCABULARY IN PICTURES

Life Events

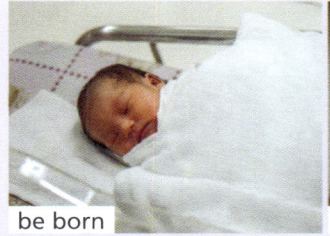

- be born
- buy a house
- get a job
- get married
- go to college
- have children
- learn to drive
- leave home
- leave school
- start school
- train to be a …
- work

Musical Instruments

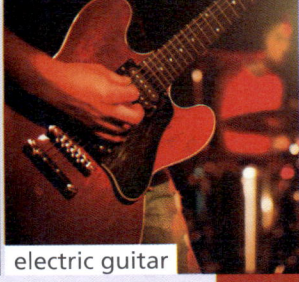

- acoustic guitar
- drums
- electric bass
- electric guitar
- flute
- keyboard
- percussion
- piano
- saxophone
- trumpet
- violin

6
ON SCREEN

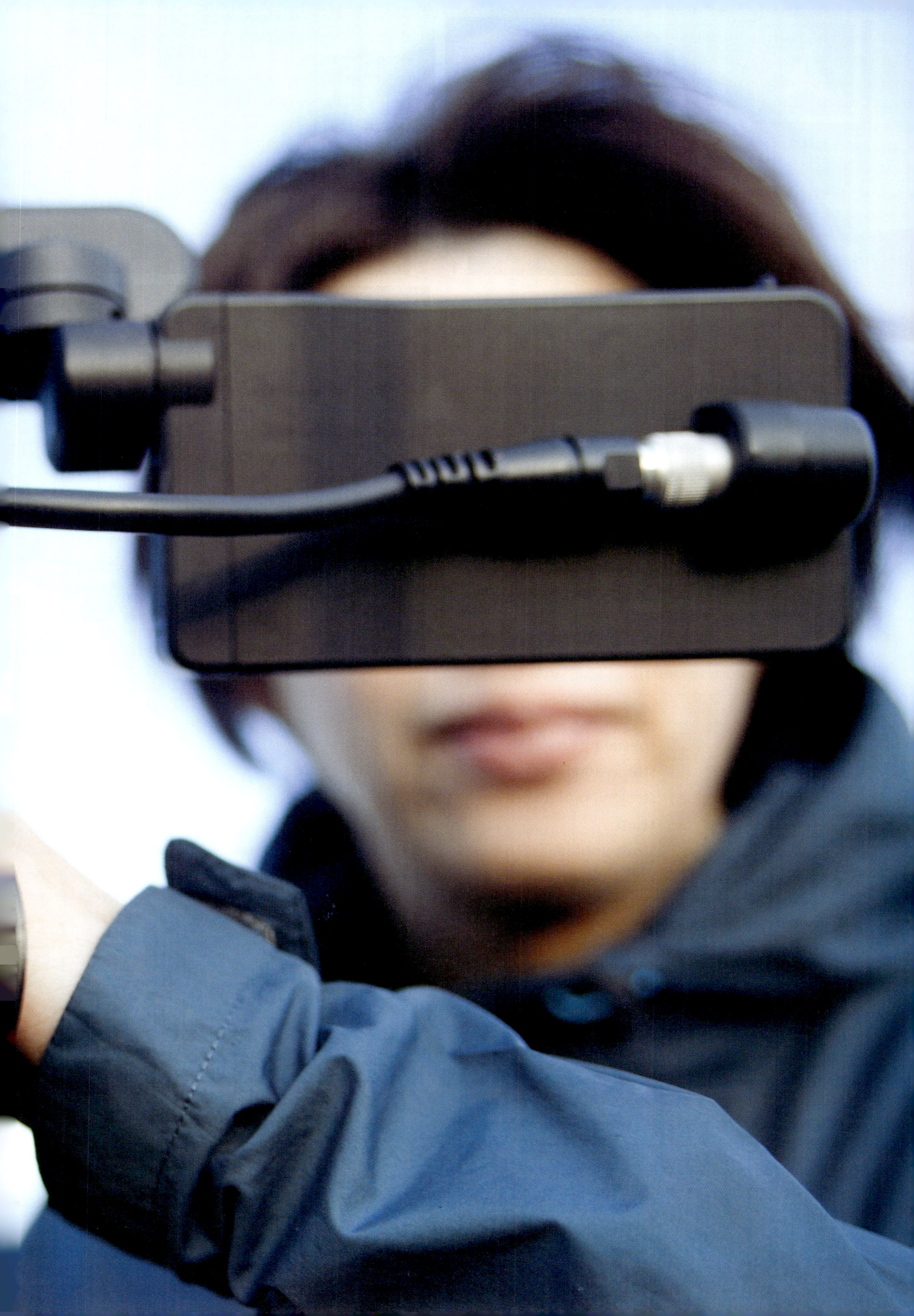

EXT. ON THE ROAD - NIGHT

The T-rex ROARS in frustration. It bends down for one final lunge at the car.

Grant sees it coming. He grabs one of the dangling fence cables on the other side of the barrier.

                    GRANT
              Grab a hold of me!

Lex wraps her arms around Grant's neck. He runs to the edge of the barrier and starts to climb down.

                    LEX
                (screaming)
              Timmy! Timmy!

VOCABULARY 1

Movies

1 Look at the words in the box. Which words can you use to describe the images?

director ☐	soundtrack ☐	
film a scene ☐	special effects ☐	
movie star ☐	star in a movie ☐	
plot ☐	streaming platform ☐	
producer ☐	stunt ☐	
release a movie ☐	stunt double ☐	
screen ☐	win an award ☐	
script ☐		

2 Listen and repeat. 🔊 52

3 Complete the chart with the words in activity 1.

people	verbs related to movies	other movie words
director	film a scene	plot

4 Complete the sentences with the correct form of the words in activity 1.

The ___director___ wants to film the action scenes tomorrow.

a The _____ is wonderful – the dialogue is great.

b The music is great too – I love the _____.

c Ariana DeBose _____ in the film. She won an _____ at the Oscars.

d A _____ does all the dangerous scenes in a movie instead of the actor.

e The _____ in that science fiction movie are wonderful. They look really realistic.

106 one hundred six

UNIT 6

📖 READING 1

1 Skim the news article. Then match predictions a-e with paragraphs 1-7.

a ☐ Will 3D movies be popular again?
b ☐ People won't stop watching movies.
c ☐ There will be human actors in the future.
d ☐ TV shows won't be interactive.
e ☐ There will be no more movie theaters.

> **READING STRATEGY**
> Look at the layout, the title, and the picture of the text in order to make some predictions about it.

Trends in Moviemaking

1 Ever since the release of the extremely popular *Avatar* in 2009, 3D movies seemed promising, but the trend didn't catch on and the number of 3D movies made each year is no longer increasing. In fact, in 2011, there were more than 60 3D movies released. In 2021, ten years later, there were fewer than 30 3D movies released. Will 3D become a trend again with the promising release of *Avatar 2: The Way of Water*? Who knows!

2 Another trend that didn't catch on was interactive TV shows on the internet. The promising idea behind interactive TV shows was that you could choose what happens, help to write the dialogue and plot, and even appear in the show! However, this trend appears to have lost its popularity.

3 On the other hand, trends like live action remakes are becoming popular. The successful *Lion King* released in 1994 gained a live action remake in 2019 directed by Jon Favreau, and *West Side Story* released in 1961 was remade in 2021 by Steven Spielberg. These new and updated versions seem to be a growing trend for the movie industry.

4 Will computer-generated images of actors replace human actors? Computer programmers can create action scenes using digital actors – they are so realistic that audiences don't realize they aren't human. This technology is very expensive, so moviemakers have decided that they are only going to use it to film dangerous stunts and to refilm some scenes. They are not going to stop using real actors, so we'll definitely have human actors for many more years!

5 Companies have already tried creating extra special effects inside the movie theater, such as smells and moving chairs, without much success. People are more interested in realistic special effects on screen. Producers are investing a lot of money to create better special effects. For this reason, the special effects are going to get more exciting and realistic – but movie theaters themselves probably won't change much.

6 Meanwhile, streaming platforms are growing more popular than ever. If people now prefer to use streaming subscriptions in the comfort of their own homes, will movie theaters disappear?

7 Since the first movie in 1895, people have loved cinema. Audiences everywhere enjoy good stories and they want entertainment. One thing is certain, people definitely won't stop watching movies!

2 🔊 53 Read and listen to the news article. Then choose the correct options.

a There is … 3D movies now compared to ten years ago.
   1 more   2 fewer

b Interactive TV shows …
   1 aren't a trend anymore.   2 is a trend.

c Live action remakes movies are becoming more …
   1 popular.   2 unpopular.

d The movie industry … in technology.
   1 didn't invest   2 invested

e Streaming platforms are …
   1 increasing.   2 decreasing.

3 Find words in the text that mean …

a a tendency (paragraph 1) _____
b the story of a movie or TV show (paragraph 2) _____
c achieves popularity and prestige (paragraph 3) _____
d people who work in the movie industry (paragraph 4) _____
e performances that people enjoy (paragraph 7) _____

> 🌐 **Cultural fact**
> Eventually *stunt double* may be substituted by *stuntman* or *stuntwoman* if you want to mention the performer's gender.

GRAMMAR 1

Future Form: *will*

1. Read the following sentences and complete the chart below with examples of use of *will* and *won't*.

   a Streaming platforms will probably increase.
   b We'll definitely have human actors for many years.
   c Movie theaters themselves probably won't change much.
   d People definitely won't stop watching movies.
   e Special effects will be much more advanced, according to experts.

will / won't
Make predictions about the future
When you are sure about something in the future
If you think something is likely to happen

2. What will movie theaters be like in the near future? Complete the text with the correct form of *will* and the verbs in parentheses.

   Nowadays and in the near future, technology
   a _____ (do away) with the old-school movie screen. Movies b _____ (not be) events to see at the movie theater for two hours. Instead, they c _____ (be) gamified and d _____ (unfold) in real time around you. You e _____ (literally / become) part of the action. Events f _____ (change) as you "act," and smells, tastes, and sensations g _____ (be) experienced live. Actors h _____ (be) your own avatars and you i _____ (turn into) a star! What about all those movie stars? What j _____ (they / do)?

3. Choose the most appropriate verb form to fill in the blanks in the sentences below.

   a In the future, there _____ lots of programs to create special effects.
      ☐ be   ☐ will be   ☐ will
   b I don't think Spielberg _____ that movie.
      ☐ won't   ☐ 'll   ☐ will direct
   c How many people _____ movies on movie theaters in ten years' time?
      ☐ will watch   ☐ watch   ☐ won't
   d _____ the soundtrack in an online platform?
      ☐ They will release   ☐ Will they release
      ☐ They won't release
   e I think that movie _____ a lot of awards.
      ☐ will win   ☐ win   ☐ will

Future Form: *be going to*

4. Read the sentences below and write (A) if they talk about future plans and intentions or (B) if there is evidence in the present for future events or actions.

   a ☐ Steven Spielberg is going to direct a remake movie.
   b ☐ Those actors are really good. They aren't going to be fired.
   c ☐ The director is going to use stunt doubles for that scene. The actors may get hurt if they shoot it.
   d ☐ Ariana DeBose is going to take a break after that movie.

5. What was used to indicate the future events in activity 4?
   _____

6. Use the words in the box to complete the chart below.

Are they going to   aren't going to use   is going to

	be going to
+	Spielberg _____ release a new movie.
−	Moviemakers _____ new technology so much.
?	_____ use stunt doubles instead of actors for that scene?

UNIT 6

7 Match a-e with 1-5 to make sentences.

a ☐ The director has asked for silence because …
b ☐ They are not going to do the stunts …
c ☐ He has earned so much money …
d ☐ I lost my purse last week so …
e ☐ Are you going to book the seats at the movie theater …

1 I'm going to buy another one.
2 filming is going to start.
3 before next Thursday?
4 because they think they are too dangerous.
5 that he is going to retire now.

8 Complete the sentences below with the correct form of the verbs in the box. Use *be going to*.

> give   invite   leave
> (not) ask   save   travel

a I love that song! I _____ it to my phone right now.
b _____ around the world during her gap year before university.
c They _____ her to sing because she has a terrible voice.
d Jim _____ the city because he didn't get the new job.
e _____ you _____ me your homework before tomorrow?
f I _____ Paul to my birthday party.

9 Choose the correct options.

a In the future, I think people **will live / are going to live** in space.
b I don't think that I **will learn / am going to learn** French in the future.
c I **will meet / am going to meet** my friends on the weekend.
d In my opinion, that movie **won't / isn't going to** win an award.
e What **will you do / are you going to do** after school today?

➡ **GRAMMAR GUIDE** page 116

PRONUNCIATION

Sentence Stress and Weak Forms

1 Listen and repeat the sentences. Which two syllables have the main stress in each sentence? What happens to the words in bold?

🔊 54

a I'm **going to** download that song.
b We're **going to** invite **them** to the party.
c They aren't **going to** buy a house.

2 Listen and repeat the sentences.

🔊 54

LISTENING

3D Movies

1 👥 INTERFACE Work in pairs. What 3D movies have you seen?

> Have you seen any 3D movies? Which ones? Did you like them?

> Yes, I have. I've seen *Le Petit Prince* and *Minions*. They were great!

2 What do you know about 3D movies? Do you think these statements are *true* (T) or *false* (F)?

a ☐ 3D technology first appeared in 1994.
b ☐ In 3D movies, two images are combined into one image to create a sensation of depth.
c ☐ The first 3D movie was for children.
d ☐ The movie *Monster House* came out in 2007.
e ☐ The movie *Beowulf* was the second 3D movie for adults.
f ☐ Even though 3D movie releases are decreasing, they still have popularity.
g ☐ TVs that can show 3D movies are a trend nowadays.

3 Listen and check your answers.

🔊 55

💬 SPEAKING

3D Movies Are Awesome!

🔊 56) Dan and Rita are talking about 3D movies. Listen and complete the dialogue.

> Rita, what **a** _____ next Saturday afternoon?

> Well, I **b** _____ to the movies. Do you want to come?

> Good idea! What are you **c** _____?

> In fact, I'm planning to go for *Dolittle* in 3D.

> You love **d** _____, don't you?

> Yeah, you know, I love fantasy, adventure … As for *Dolittle*, I've read **e** _____ Tom Holland doing the voice for Jip, Dr. Dolittle's dog … And we **f** _____ to see Robert Downey Jr. as Dr. Dolittle. I **g** _____ emotional when I see him. I liked him so much in *Avengers: Endgame*.

> It sounds awesome!

> 3D movies are the most spectacular way to enjoy some big-screen thrills, in my opinion. That's why I like them!

> The only problem is that tickets for **h** _____ are a bit expensive …

> I know, but some of these **i** _____ are worth watching anyway!

FUNCTIONAL LANGUAGE

Going to the Movies

What are you doing … ?
You like …, don't you?
I love …
What are you going to watch?
What do you want to see?

Speaking Task

Plan a dialogue about movie preferences between you and a classmate.

■ Step 1

What kind of movies do you like? Choose one of your favorite movies to talk about.

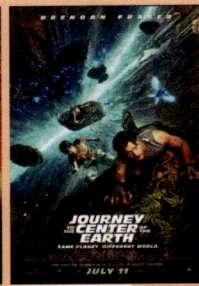

action   adventure   animated

■ Step 2

Plan questions about movies your classmate would like to watch.

Would you like to go to the movies?
What about watching … ?
What are you doing … ?
What are you going to watch?

Plan what your classmate is going to say.

I don't know. I think I'll …
I like …
I'd love to see …
I'm planning …
I'd like to see …
I'll probably …

■ Step 3

Work in pairs. Take turns practicing the dialogue.

UNIT 6

CULTURE

Steven Spielberg

Steven Allan Spielberg is one of the finest Hollywood directors in the history of the movie industry and also one of the founding pioneers of the new Hollywood era. He has directed many popular and significant movies in the recent Hollywood history, such as *E.T. the Extra-Terrestrial*, *Jurassic Park*, *Close Encounters of the Third Kind*, *Schindler's List*, and *Saving Private Ryan*. In a career spanning more than four decades, Spielberg's movies have covered many themes and genres (science fiction, action-adventure, and high drama).

Is he thinking about retiring? No way! Spielberg likes to stay busy. He is either planning his next step as an iconic moviemaker, thinking about the next massive blockbuster, or producing something we'll probably watch and enjoy immensely.

Nowadays, Spielberg is working on some upcoming movies. *The Fabelmans* will be released in 2022. *Maestro*, *Transformers: Rise of the Beasts*, *Indiana Jones 5*, and *The Color Purple* are going to be released in 2023. Spielberg is definitely a genius moviemaker, and his legacy is memorable.

1 Read and listen to the information about Steven Spielberg and complete the chart.

57))

Steven Spielberg	
Job	
Famous movies	
Movie genres	
Plans for the future	

2 Think of a famous person in the movie industry in your country (a director, an actor, etc.) and fill in the chart below.

Name:	
Job	
Famous movies	
Movie genres	
Plans for the future	

VOCABULARY 2

Suffixes -ion and -ment

1 Complete the chart with the verbs in the box. Then make the verbs into nouns by adding the suffixes -ion or -ment.

> advertise argue compete connect
> decorate develop educate enjoy equip
> excite inform possess predict suggest

verbs	nouns -ion
compete	competition

verbs	nouns -ment
advertise	advertisement

2 Listen and repeat.
58))

3 Complete the sentences with nouns from activity 1.

I don't know what to write in the script. Do you have a good s___suggestion____?

a You need a lot of e_____ to make a movie.
b What is the c_____ between these two things?
c I think e_____ is important. I want to get a good job, so I study a lot.
d Can you send me some i_____ about the movie course?
e I get a lot of e_____ from reading – I love it!

4 Complete the questions with nouns from activity 1.

What's your favorite ___possession___?

a What's the funniest _____ on TV in your opinion?
b Do you put up _____ at Christmas?
c When was the last time you had an _____? Why did you argue?
d Do you need any special _____ to go camping?

5 **INTERFACE** Work in pairs. Ask and answer the questions in activity 4.

> What's your favorite possession?

> My favorite possession is my family's photo album. It seems like the story from a movie.

TIP

Use your dictionary to find out how the suffix -less changes the meaning of these nouns: use, help, job, home.

UNIT 6

READING 2

1 Skim the advertisement. Then choose the correct options.

   a Fresh Films has a competition for **teenagers** / **directors**.
   b The winners make a movie with **new actors** / **Hollywood stars**.

Make a Movie in Hollywood!

Many teenagers only dream of making a movie or becoming the next big name in Hollywood. Fresh Films gives some of them the opportunity to do exactly that! Fresh Films is opening a moviemaking competition soon. This film school is giving those teens the training, equipment, and connections to make their dreams come true. They are inviting talented teens to spend a week in Hollywood in December. The competition is open to anyone aged 13-19. All you have to do is explain why the organizers should choose you.
If they choose you, you'll spend a week in Hollywood and you'll produce, film, and edit movies with real Hollywood movie stars!
Sixteen-year-old Gina has always wanted to be a moviemaker and she is registering for the competition tomorrow. "If I am successful, I'll get to work with professionals. It's a fantastic opportunity! I really want to go to film school, but my parents want me to go to college. They'll let me go to film school if I win, I'm sure."
Since it started in 2002, the Fresh Films competition for teens has produced over 80 movies and shown movies at over 20 festivals. Some of the past winners now have careers in movies.

So, what are you waiting for?
There's still time to apply!
You never know, you could soon be on your way to Hollywood!

2 Read and listen. Check your answers.
🔊 59

3 Read the text again. Then write T for *true* or F for *false*. Correct the false sentences.

   a ☐ This is the first year Fresh Films has organized the competition.
   _____
   _____

   b ☐ To be chosen, you must convince the organizers that you deserve it.
   _____
   _____

   c ☐ Gina is one of the teenagers chosen to spend a week in Hollywood.
   _____
   _____

   d ☐ Gina's parents think she should go to college, not to film school.
   _____
   _____

   e ☐ All of the movies made by teenagers have been in movie festivals.
   _____
   _____

4 👥 **INTERFACE** Work in pairs. Imagine that your classmate works at Fresh Films. Try to convince him or her to choose you for the competition.

> Why do you want to train at our film school?

> I love horror movies. I have great ideas for a super scary movie!

one hundred thirteen **113**

GRAMMAR 2

Review: Present Progressive for Future Arrangements

1 Read the following sentences. Underline the verb and circle the time expression.

   a Fresh Films is opening a moviemaking competition soon.

   b They are inviting talented teens to spend a week in Hollywood in December.

   c This film school is giving those teens the training, equipment, and connections to make their dreams come true.

   d Sixteen-year-old Gina is registering for the competition tomorrow.

2 Complete the rules for the use of the present progressive for future arrangements. Use the words in the box.

| always   future arrangements   It is not |
| organization   plan |

   a An arrangement is a _____ decided between two people or a person and a group of people, an _____, or a company.

   b _____ necessary to state who the arrangement is with.

   c Time expressions are often (but not _____) used when the present progressive is used to talk about _____.

3 Complete the sentences with the correct form of the words in parentheses. Use the present progressive.

   a Tomorrow I _____ (travel) to the festival by train.

   b _____ you _____ (give) me a lift to the station?

   c My friend Alex _____ (meet) me at 11am.

   d I _____ (not take) the 10am train.

   e _____ we _____ (eat) before I leave?

4 Complete the text with the verbs in parentheses in the present progressive.

Singaporeans **a** _____ (take part) in a moviemaking competition until the end of the month. Who **b** _____ (encourage) them to make movies? Moviemakers from a community independent event! The competition co-chairman **c** _____ (expect) lots of entries. Eligible residents **d** _____ (make) movies that are no longer than 10 minutes. They **e** _____ (not film) with professional cameras; they **f** _____ (use) their smartphones. Those Singaporeans who only speak English are invited too!

5 **INTERFACE** Work in pairs. Ask and answer questions about your plans for the weekend. Ask about Friday night, Saturday morning, and Saturday night.

> Are you doing anything on Saturday morning?

> Yes! I'm planning a brunch for my cousins. They are coming for my sister's wedding on Sunday.

➡ **GRAMMAR GUIDE** page 116

WRITING

A Movie Review

① EXPLORING THE CONTEXT

1 Skim the movie review on page 115.

   a Where was it published?
   _____

   b Where else can you find movie reviews?
   _____
   _____

   c Do you need to be a professional critic to write a movie review?
   _____

2 Read the movie review and listen. Does the writer like the movie? _____

UNIT 6

3 Read the review again and match descriptions a-d with paragraphs 1-4.

a ☐ conclusion: your opinion and recommendation

b ☐ information about what was good about the movie and what was the best thing

c ☐ introduction: general information, director's name, actors' names, when the movie came out

d ☐ information about the story

---

www.filmfans.com

The Film Fans Blog
Our community of film fans want to know: What's your favorite movie? Write your review (120-150 words) and we'll publish it!

by Ryan_13

My Favorite Movie

1. One of my favorite movies is *Black Panther*. It's a superhero movie that came out in 2018. The director was Ryan Coogler and he co-wrote the script with Joe Robert Cole. The main actors are Chadwick Boseman, Michael B. Jordan, and Lupita Nyong'o. *Black Panther* was one of the last works by Boseman, who sadly died in 2020 due to cancer.
2. The plot is based on the Marvel Comics story about T'Challa, who became the king of Wakanda – a technologically advanced nation in Africa – after his father's death. He must fight against an enemy who also wants to be the king of Wakanda. For me, *Black Panther* is one of the best Marvel movies.
3. The actors were very good. I thought the soundtrack (by Ludwig Göransson) was also amazing. I think the best thing about the movie is the computer-generated images – they are really fantastic. It's a 3D movie and you really feel like you are part of the action.
4. In my opinion, *Black Panther* is a great movie. The special effects are awesome and it also makes you think. I would recommend it to everyone.

② PLANNING

1. Write a movie review for *The Film Fans Blog*. Think about your favorite movie.

Take notes on the setting, plot, actors, soundtrack, and special effects.

2. If necessary, look up information about the movie on the internet.

LANGUAGE FOCUS

Giving Opinions

One of my favorite movies is *Black Panther*.
For me, it is one of the best Marvel movies.
I think the best thing about the movie is the computer-generated images.
In my opinion, *Black Panther* is a great movie.

1. Order the words to make sentences.

a I / very / the / was / script / funny / thought
_____
_____

b I / think / the / thing / was / the plot / best / about / the movie
_____
_____

c to / recommend / I / it / everyone / would
_____
_____

d it / a / great / In / opinion, / movie / my / is
_____
_____

③ WRITING

Write a first draft. Organize your information into four paragraphs.

④ CHECKING & EDITING

1. Read your movie review and check:
   - Did I express my opinion clearly?
   - Did I summarize the plot without giving away the ending?
   - Did I discuss important aspects of the movie (direction, acting, soundtrack)?
   - Did I point out the things I like (or don't like)?
   - Have I included a conclusion making a recommendation to the reader?

2. Perfect your work and write a final copy.

⑤ SHARING

1. Share your movie review with your classmates. You can do this with hard copies or digital copies.

2. Read your classmates' reviews. What are the class's favorite movies? Which of the reviewed movies do you want to watch?

GRAMMAR GUIDE

Future Form: *will*

+	I / You / He / She / It / We / You / They	**'ll** go.
−	I / You / He / She / It / We / You / They	**won't** go.

?	**Will** I / you / he / she / it / we / you / they	**go**?
	Yes, I / you / he / she / it / we / you / they **will**. No, I / you / he / she / it / we / you / they **won't**.	

- we use *will / won't* + the main verb in the base form to make predictions about the future
  I think that movie **will** win a lot of awards.
- we can use *definitely* when we are certain about something in the future and *probably* when we think something is likely
  That movie **definitely** won't win any awards!
  Most movies will **probably** be on streaming platforms in future.

Future Form: *be going to*

+	I	**'m going to** come.
	You	**'re going to** come.
	He / She / It	**'s going to** come.
	We / You / They	**'re going to** come.

−	I	**'m not going to** come.
	You	**aren't going to** come.
	He / She / It	**isn't going to** come.
	We / You / They	**aren't going to** come.

?	**Is** he / she / it **going to** come? Yes, he / she / it **is**. / No, he / she / it **isn't**. **Are** you / we / they **going to** come? Yes, you / we / they **are**. No, you / we / they **aren't**.

- we use *be going to* to talk about future intentions
- we also use *be going to* when there is evidence in the present that something is very likely to happen
- we form sentences with *be* + (*not*) + *going to* + the main verb in the base form
  They **aren't going to** watch a movie.

Review: Present Progressive for Future Arrangements

- we use the present progressive for definite plans and arrangements in the future
- we use it with future time expressions, such as *this evening, tomorrow, on Friday, next week*
  I'm **meeting my friends on Friday**.
- we form the present progressive with *be* + main verb + *-ing*

PROGRESS CHECK

Name: _____
Class name / Period: _____
Teacher: _____
Date: _____

Movies

1 Complete the sentences with the words in the box.

> awards   plot   screen   script   soundtrack

   a Can you move your head? I can't see the _____.

   b Who wrote the _____ for that movie? The dialogue is really funny.

   c Tom Holland has won many _____, including MTV Movie & TV Award for Best Performance in a Movie in 2022, for his character in *Spider-Man: No Way Home*.

   d The _____ of that movie was confusing. It's a very complicated story.

   e The music in that movie was great. I loved the _____.

Suffixes *-ion* and *-ment*

2 Complete the sentences with the correct form of the words in parentheses.

   a I didn't agree with him and we had an _____ (argue) about it.

   b If you need any more _____ (inform), just ask me.

   c What is your favorite _____ (advertise) on TV?

   d Does anyone have a good _____ (suggest) about where to go tonight?

Future Form: *will*

3 Complete the sentences with the correct form of *will*.

   a Where do you think you _____ (live) in the future?

   b That movie definitely _____ (not win) an award. It is terrible!

   c Do you think they _____ (make) another movie together?

   d Perhaps they _____ (film) those scenes in Scotland, I'm not sure.

   e _____ (he / write) the music for the movie?

Future Form: *be going to*

4 Order the words to make sentences and questions.

   a going / be / hot / It's / to / today
   _____
   _____

   b not / going / tonight / I'm / go out / to
   _____
   _____

   c they / to England / Are / to / going / fly ?
   _____
   _____

Review: Present Progressive for Future Arrangements

5 Make sentences and questions with the words below.

   a What / you / do / next weekend?
   _____
   _____

   b He / not study / Chinese / tomorrow.
   _____
   _____

   c Where / you / stay / during vacation?
   _____
   _____

Grammar Buildup 6

1 2 3 4 5 6 7 8

6 Complete the interview with the correct form of the verbs in parentheses.

Interviewer Congratulations on your new movie. Do you think
a _____ (it / win) an award?

Monica Thanks. I hope it will get a nomination.

Interviewer What b _____ (you / do) if you win?

Monica If I win, I c _____ (celebrate) with my friends.

Interviewer And what about your plans for the future? What
d _____ (you / do) next?

Monica I e _____ (start) work on a new movie next week. After that, I'm not sure. Perhaps I
f _____ (take) a vacation!

UNIT 6

VOCABULARY IN PICTURES

Movies

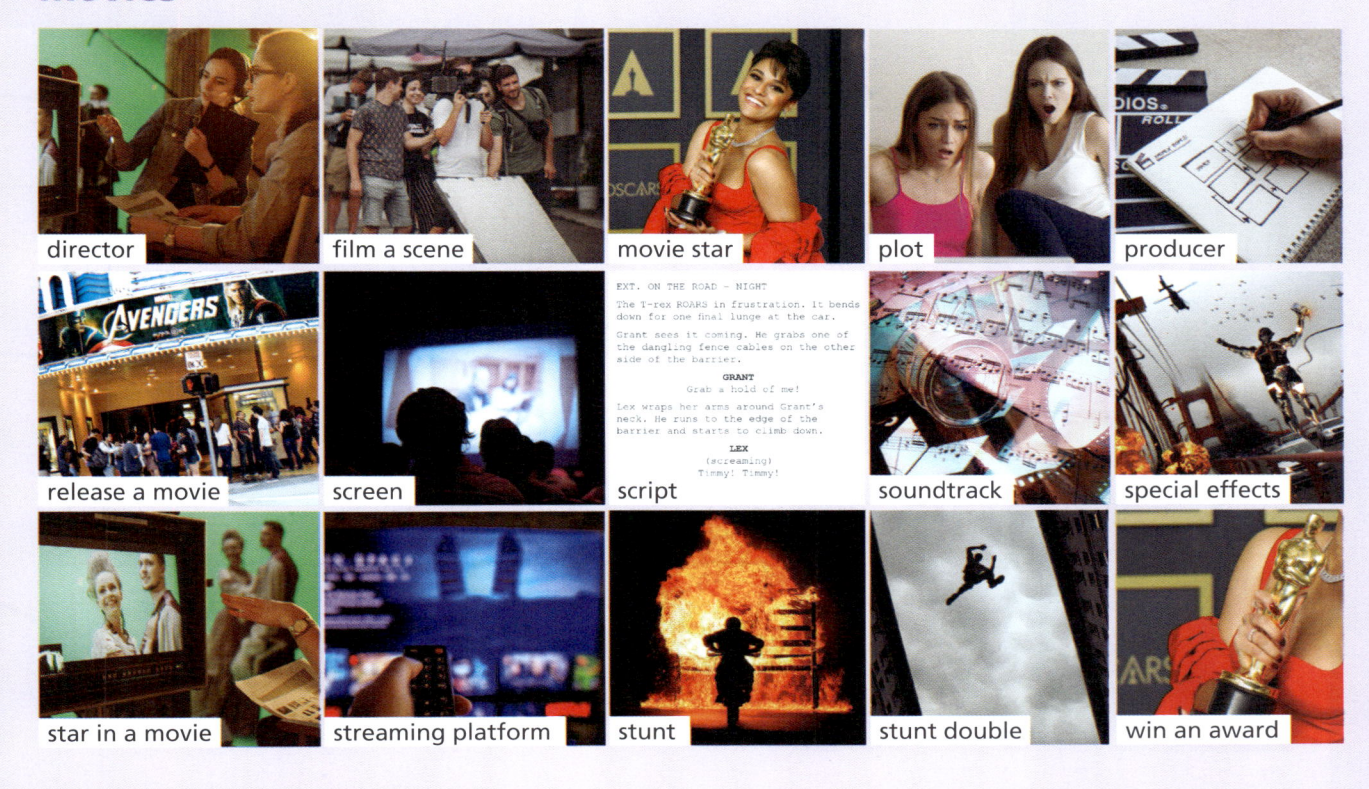

- director
- film a scene
- movie star
- plot
- producer
- release a movie
- screen
- script
- soundtrack
- special effects
- star in a movie
- streaming platform
- stunt
- stunt double
- win an award

Suffixes *-ion* and *-ment*

- advertisement
- argument
- competition
- connection
- decoration
- development
- education
- enjoyment
- equipment
- excitement
- information
- possession
- prediction
- suggestion

REVIEW 3

VOCABULARY

Start

1 Which **A** tries to sell you things?
a ___ ___ ___ ___ ___ ___ ___ ___ ___ ___ ___

6 Which **C** involves people or teams and has a winner?
c ___ ___ ___ ___ ___ ___ ___ ___ ___ ___

7 Which **P** is to guess the future?
p ___ ___ ___ ___ ___ ___ ___ ___

13 Which **E** are often special in movies?
e ___ ___ ___ ___ ___ ___

12 Which **B** is an electric musical instrument with four strings?
b ___ ___ ___

14 Which **C** do you can go to when you finish high school?
c ___ ___ ___ ___ ___ ___

19 Which **S** is the written text of a movie?
s ___ ___ ___ ___ ___

18 Which **K** is the electric equivalent to a piano?
k ___ ___ ___ ___ ___ ___ ___

Finish

120 one hundred twenty

2 Which **H** do you leave when you become independent?
h ___ ___ ___

3 Which **T** is a music instrument?
t ___ ___ ___ ___ ___ ___

5 Which **D** is a percussion instrument you play with two sticks?
d ___ ___ ___ ___

4 Which **P** is the story of a movie?
p ___ ___ ___

8 Which **A** can a movie win?
a ___ ___ ___ ___

9 Which **F** is a musical instrument that you blow?
f ___ ___ ___ ___

11 Which **S** is the music of a movie?
s ___ ___ ___ ___ ___ ___ ___ ___ ___

10 Which **S** do you start to learn different subjects?
s ___ ___ ___ ___ ___

15 Which **G** is an musical instrument with six strings?
g ___ ___ ___ ___ ___

16 Which **D** do you need to have a license of to use a car?
d ___ ___ ___ ___

17 Which **I** means knowledge or facts about something?
i ___ ___ ___ ___ ___ ___ ___ ___ ___ ___

one hundred twenty-one 121

REVIEW 3

GRAMMAR

will / won't

1 Complete the sentences with *will* and the verbs in the box.

~~be~~   eat   feel   get   leave   play

I _____'ll be_____ an actor when I'm older.

a My sister _____ home soon.

b I _____ married when I'm 30.

c You _____ tired tomorrow morning.

d Jack _____ the guitar in a famous band one day.

e We _____ pasta when we go to Italy.

2 Write complete sentences with *won't* and the verbs in parentheses.

We ___won't have___ a good time on the beach. It's cold. (have)

a I _____ as a doctor because I don't like needles very much. (work)

b My best friend _____ dancing because she's ill. (go)

c My family _____ by plane. It's very expensive. (travel)

d You _____ your exams. You always study a lot. (fail)

e Your cousin _____ the movie. It's a western. (like)

f It _____ cold tomorrow. It's summer. (be)

3 Choose the correct answers to complete the sentences.

My brother's only eight. He'll get married …
1 soon.   **2** next month.   **3** <u>one day.</u>

a It's March. We'll finish school …
1 next week.   **2** in June.   **3** tomorrow.

b I'm 14. I won't leave school …
1 tomorrow.   **2** one day.   **3** when I'm older.

c My sister loves talking. She'll be a sign language interpreter …
1 tomorrow.   **2** when she's older.   **3** soon.

d The best player on my team has a broken leg. We won't win the game …
1 next week.   **2** one day.   **3** soon.

e It's snowing a lot. School will be closed …
1 one day.   **2** tomorrow.   **3** in May.

4 Write questions and short answers about Jess', Tom's, Fred's, and Julia's future.

	Jess	Tom	Fred and Julia
transportation	motorcycle	fast car	bicycle
job	engineer	nurse	actor
home	Paris	London	Hollywood

Jess / drive / a fast car
Will Jess drive a fast car?
No, she won't.

a Tom / work / as a nurse?
_____
_____

b Jess / study / to be an engineer?
_____
_____

c Fred and Julia / ride / a bicycle?
_____
_____

d Jess / live / in Hollywood?
_____
_____

e Fred and Julia / live / in Paris?
_____
_____

First Conditional

5 Write sentences with the first conditional. Add commas when needed.

If / Mike / fail / his exams / his dad / be / angry
If Mike fails his exams, his dad will be angry.

a Our teacher / be / happy / if / we / tidy / our desks
_____

b If / the sun / shines / we / go / to the lake
_____

c If / mom / not come / home soon / I / cook / dinner
_____

d We / cross / the Atlantic / if / we / sail / to New York
_____

Future Tense: *will*

6 Write predictions for the future with *will* or *won't*. Include the words in parentheses.

streaming platforms / increase (probably)
Streaming platforms will probably increase.

a My brother / be / a movie star (definitely)
_____

b That movie / not win / an award (definitely)
_____

c Schoolchildren / not use / books (probably)
_____

7 Write questions with *will*. Then write true short answers.

(your dad) be prime minister
Will your dad be prime minister?
No, he won't.

a (you and your friends) film a scene
_____
_____

b (you) go out for a meal on Saturday
_____
_____

c (your school) be open tomorrow
_____
_____

Future Tense: *be going to*

8 Complete the sentences with the correct form of *be going to* and the verbs in parentheses.

They're _____going to build_____ a new movie theater. (build)

a I _____ any more online movies. (not buy)

b Look out! Your book _____ on the floor. (fall)

c _____ Sara _____ as a stunt double? (work)

d Matt _____ math at college. (not study)

Present Progressive for Future Arrangements

9 Look at Kate's diary and complete the sentences about her weekend. Use the present progressive.

Kate has a lot of arrangements this weekend.

Saturday		Sunday	
10am	play tennis with Dan	11am	Grandma & Grandpa come
2pm	meet friends in town	3pm	do a sponsored swim
7pm	go out for a pizza with Emma	6pm	watch a movie at Joe's house

She _'s playing tennis_ with Dan at 10 o'clock on Saturday. In the afternoon, she
a _____. Then, in the evening, Emma and Kate **b** _____.
On Sunday morning, Kate's grandparents
c _____. Kate **d** _____ at 3 o'clock that afternoon, and then at 6 o'clock she
e _____ at Joe's house.

DIGITAL LITERACY

How to Select Sources of Information

Why Was It Made?

CLIMATE CRISIS
If we don't reduce the use of fossil fuels ...

But it's OK to use fossil fuels! I just saw a video that said ...

There you go with your videos again, Dan ...

Do you know how to evaluate a source of information, son?

Sure! I check the author's credentials. I also check if the information is supported by evidence ...

All this is very good. But there's a key question you should ask ...

What is the purpose of this information? Why was it made? The video you saw may have been made by an organization that is biased ...

"It was made by an organization called AFFP ..."

Let me see what that means ... Association of Fossil Fuel Producers!

Oh! That source is definitely biased!

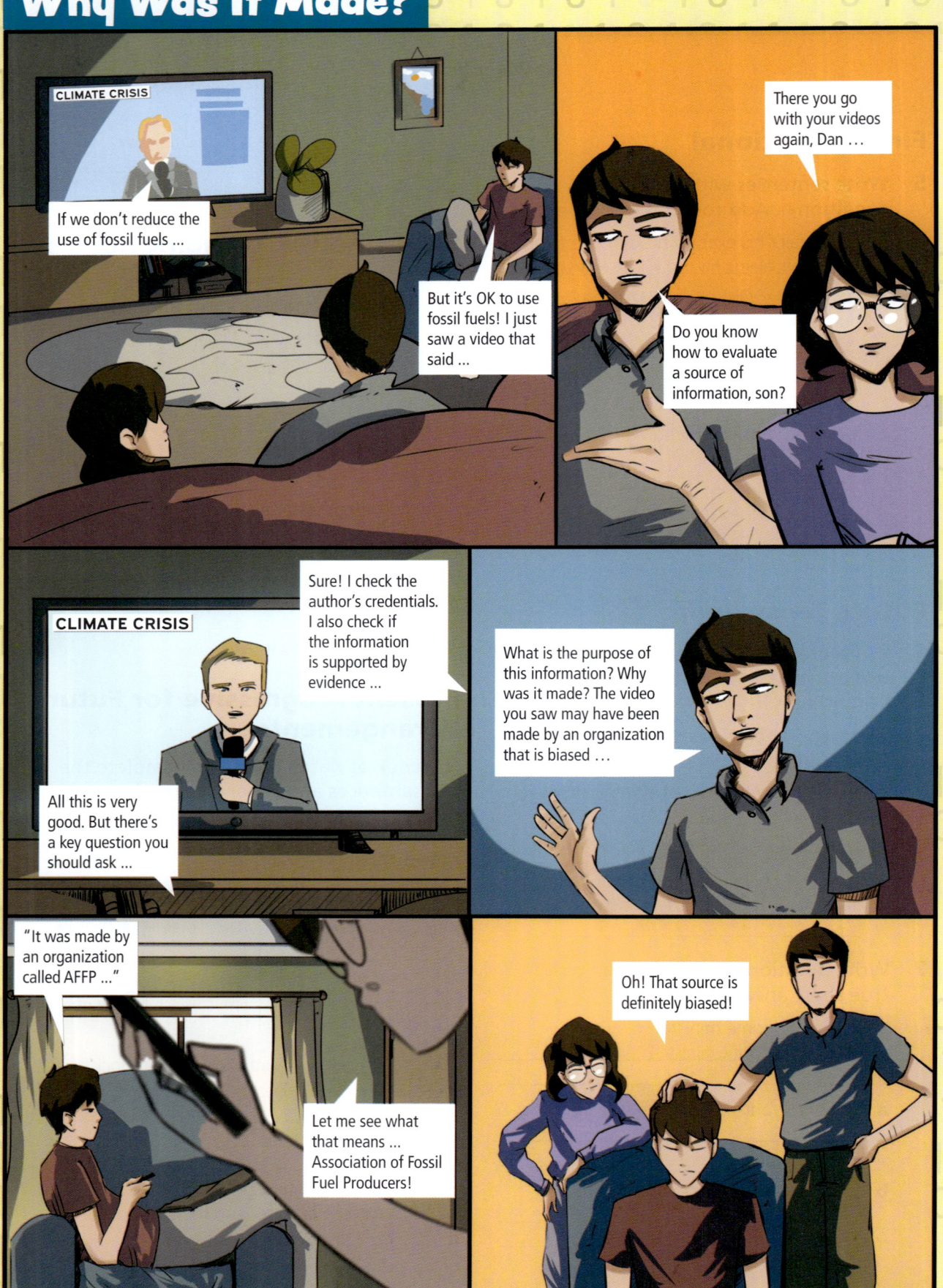

124 one hundred twenty-four

1 Read and listen. Then answer the questions.

🔊 61

a Why is the video watched by Daniel biased?
_____
_____

b Why was the video made?
_____
_____

2 Below are some questions you should ask when selecting information sources. Check (✓) the questions that Daniel asked and cross (✗) the one that he did not ask. Which ones are not mentioned in the story?

a Is the information relevant? Does it relate to your topic? ☐

b How current is the information? ☐

c Who is the author? Is he or she an authority on the subject? ☐

d How accurate is the content? Is it supported by factual evidence? ☐

e Is the source biased? Does it promote a product or an ideology? ☐

f How professional is the source's website? Is it free of typos? ☐

3 In groups, choose a topic you are currently studying in any school subject. Look for sources of information on this topic and apply the checklist from activity 2 to each of them.

4 Choose two sources of information, one reliable (passes the checklist) and the other unreliable (fails the checklist).

5 Show these two sources of information to the other groups, without saying which is which. Ask them to tell you which one is reliable and for what reasons.

a Did different groups have the same opinion on the sources?

b If there are differences, discuss the reasons together.

one hundred twenty-five **125**

7

THE WORLD WE LIVE IN

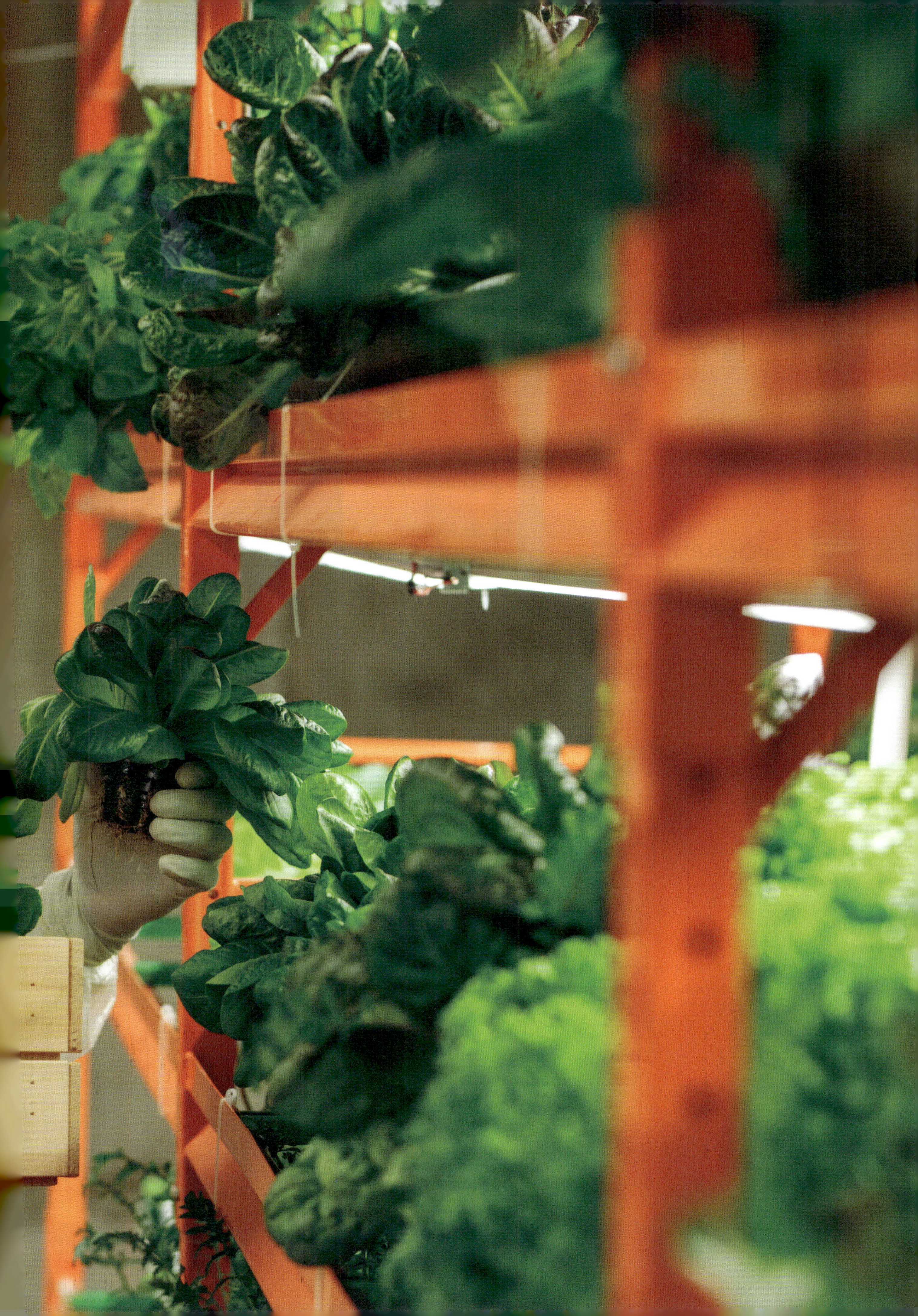

VOCABULARY 1

Materials and Containers

1 Look at the words in the box. Which of the words are containers (C)? Which are materials (M)?

aluminum ☐	cotton ☐
bag ☐	glass ☐
bottle ☐	jar ☐
box ☐	metal ☐
can ☐	paper ☐
cardboard ☐	plastic ☐
carton ☐	wool ☐

2 Listen and repeat.

62))

3 Match the words in activity 1 with pictures 1-11. Some items have more than one answer.

a ☐ aluminum   h ☐ cotton
b ☐ bag   i ☐ glass
c ☐ bottle   j ☐ jar
d ☐ box   k ☐ metal
e ☐ can   l ☐ paper
f ☐ cardboard m ☐ plastic
g ☐ carton   n ☐ wool

4 Complete the sign with words from activity 1.

Welcome to Red Forest Recycling Center

The BLUE bin is for
a _____ and
b _____.
Put your boxes and newspapers in here!

The YELLOW bin is for
c _____ and
d _____.
All your cans and plastic bags go here.

The GREEN bin is for
e _____.
Use this for bottles and jars.

The BROWN bin is for clothes.
Please wash your
f _____ T-shirts and
g _____ sweaters first.

128   one hundred twenty-eight

UNIT 7

📖 READING 1

1 Skim the text below. What do the entrants' texts express?

　a　tips
　b　testimonials

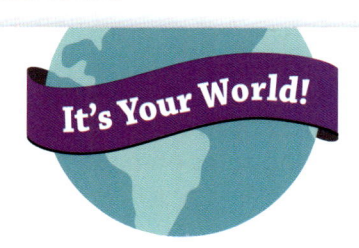

It's Your World!

Every year for five years we've organized the It's Your World! competition for under-16s to give tips to save the planet. This year, Imran Chopra is our winner, with Jake Burns and Leanne Morris as runners-up. Their tips are simple but effective – have a look! Congratulations to Imran, Jake, and Leanne!

Theme: Reduce, refuse, reuse, recycle

How many hours have you spent outside today? Outdoor activities are healthier than indoor entertainment and they save electricity. If you reduce your "screen time," you'll do your planet a favor.
So switch off lights, the TV, and gaming consoles and get out there!
Imran Chopra, Eureka, CA

"I haven't worn this for years!" You haven't? Don't throw away old clothes. Put everything into two piles: clothes someone can wear and clothes no one can wear. Take the first pile to thrift shops or give them to friends. Take the rest to a recycling center. You can also reuse wool or cotton clothes to clean your house with.
Jake Burns, Erie, PA

Refuse to buy products with a lot of plastic! Even better, write to the company and explain why you haven't bought their product. Also, when you buy food (for example, chocolate or cans of soft drinks), look for the Fairtrade symbol or support local companies. This is better for the environment and helps local communities.
Leanne Morris, Pueblo, CO

2 🔊 63 Read and listen. Match the people with the words.

　a　Imran　　　☐ reuse and recycle
　b　Jake　　　 ☐ refuse
　c　Leanne　　☐ reduce

3 Scan the text. Then write T for *true* or F for *false*.

　a　☐ The It's Your World! competition is for people younger than 16.
　b　☐ Imran suggests an alternative way to generate electricity.
　c　☐ Jake gives three suggestions for old clothes.
　d　☐ Leanne tells you to write to companies and ask them to recycle plastic.
　e　☐ All three entrants ask you to reduce how much you consume of something.

4 Answer the questions.

　a　What does Imran want people to do?
　　_____
　　_____

　b　What does Jake want people to do?
　　_____
　　_____

　c　What does Leanne want people to do?
　　_____
　　_____

READING STRATEGY
Learning the meaning of prefixes like *re-* can help you guess the meaning of a word. The context around the word will help you too.

5 Check the meaning of the words in the box below. Then use them to create statements that are true for you.

rebuild　resend　restart　rewrite

_____
_____
_____
_____
_____
_____

6 ✋ **CLASS VOTE** Which of the three tips in the text do you think is the best?

one hundred twenty-nine　129

GRAMMAR 1

Present Perfect (Affirmative and Negative)

1 Look at the following sentences and underline the verb form.

  a Some children have spent too many hours in front of the TV.
  b My mom has given our old clothes to charity organizations.
  c I have tried to be eco-friendly.
  d We have organized a recycling event.

2 Complete the following chart with the words in the box. Refer back to the rules in items a-e.

| has   He   've bought   've organized |

affirmative form	
I / You	_____ some Fairtrade coffee.
_____ / She / (It)	_____ reduced his / her / (its) screen time.
We / You / They	_____ a recycling event.

  a We form the present perfect with *have* (I / you / we / they) or *has* (he / she / it) + the past participle of the main verb.
  b The past participle of regular verbs is formed by adding *-d* or *-ed* to the main verb.
  c Some verbs have irregular past participles.
  d *'ve* is the contracted form of *have* and *'s* is the contracted form of *has*.
  e The present perfect is used to express an action that happened at an indefinite time in the past but is important at the time of speaking.

3 Complete the sentences with the present perfect form of the verbs in parentheses. Use the spelling rules on page 138 to help you.

  a I_____ (recycle) my old clothes.
  b She_____ (decide) to recycle at school.
  c My father_____ (try) a new organic shampoo.
  d We_____ (reduce) our screen time.

4 Complete the text with the present perfect form of the verbs in parentheses.

> Eco-tourism **a** _____ (become) quite popular in the last few years. People **b** _____ (build) eco-hotels all over the world. The public reaction **c** _____ (be) very positive. The hotels **d** _____ (provide) 100 percent organic cotton towels and they **e** _____ (use) solar energy for their visitors. In general, water and electricity consumption in the hotels **f** _____ (fall).

5 Write complete sentences. Use the present perfect affirmative form.

a They / turn off / all the lights.
_____
_____

b She / pass / the exam.
_____
_____

c She / break / the window.
_____
_____

d The boy / eat / all the chocolate.
_____
_____

e He / steal / the car.
_____
_____

f He / throw away / the old toys.
_____
_____

UNIT 7

6 *Hasn't / has not* and *haven't / have not* are the negative forms of *has* and *have* respectively. Complete the chart below.

negative form
I / You _____ purchased anything new in the past month.
He / She / (It) _____ worn that T-shirt anymore.
We / You / They _____ bought any plastic products recently.

7 Choose the correct words.

   a We **haven't / hasn't** had meat for lunch today.
   b My school **haven't / hasn't** stopped using paper.
   c I **haven't / hasn't** tried Fairtrade chocolate.
   d My friends **haven't / hasn't** left school.

8 Write sentences that are true for you using the present perfect affirmative and negative form. Use the words in the box or your own ideas.

   eat   finish   read   see   visit

   I haven't finished that series.
   _____
   _____
   _____
   _____
   _____

9 **INTERFACE** Work in pairs. Compare your sentences in activity 8.

   I haven't finished that series.

   Lost in Space? I loved it!!!

➡ **GRAMMAR GUIDE** page 138

LISTENING

Eco Family

Eco Family Reduces Garbage to One Can a Year

1 Look at the headline. What do you think the radio show is about?
_____
_____

2 Listen and check your answer to activity 1.
64 🔊

3 Listen again. Then write T for *true* or F for *false*.
64 🔊

   a ☐ The family has started growing vegetables.
   b ☐ The family is vegetarian.
   c ☐ The local stores give them special plastic boxes.
   d ☐ They put used coffee grounds in the garden.
   e ☐ The family gives old toys to hospitals.

4 Answer the questions.

   a Where does the Carter family live?
   _____

   b Where do they buy their food?
   _____

   c What do they do with their old clothes?
   _____

Cultural fact

Did you know that high-income countries produce the most waste per person? Canada leads the statistics (over 1,000kg per person per year), followed by Bulgaria, The USA, Estonia, and Finland.

SPEAKING

A Fundraising Bike Ride

Ed and Adam are talking about a bike ride for a charity. Listen and complete the dialogue.

> You know, Adam, a _____ to take part in the ReCycle event which is going to happen next month.

> What is it for?

> It is to b _____ for children with cancer.

> Cool! How is it organized?

> They say on this website that, this year, the organizers c _____ a route of 15 miles. They carry your gear and provide d _____ and food along the way.

> Let me check! Look, some riders e _____ it for over 10 years! Besides helping, they f _____ lots of fun. Many of them g _____ much farther than ever imagined … Cyclists and volunteers on the way cheer and encourage the group rides.

> It sounds great!

> The only thing is that it requires lots of training …

> Yeah, but pedaling for a h _____ is a rewarding experience …

> You're right … Well, let's go for it, then!

FUNCTIONAL LANGUAGE

Talking about Charity Events

I've decided to take part in …
What is it for?
When is it?
How is it organized?

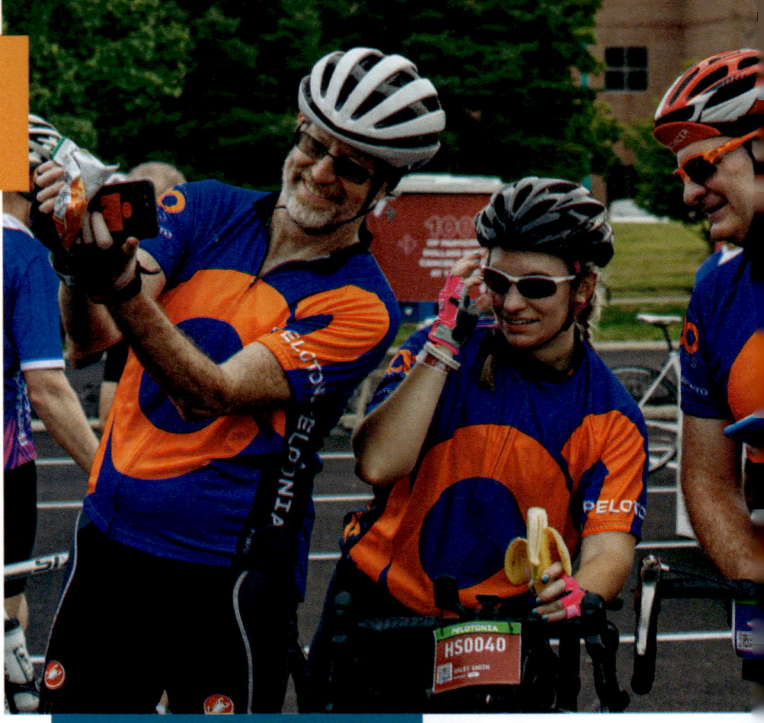

Speaking Task

Create a dialogue between you and a classmate.

Step 1

Plan about a fundraising event to take part in. Here are some examples:

A walking fundraising event

A race event

Step 2

Talk to your classmate about the event.

I've decided to take part in …
It is for …
The organizers …
Many people have taken part / helped …

Think about what your classmate is going to ask.

What is it for?
When is it?
How is it organized?

Step 3

Take turns practicing the dialogue.

CULTURE

New Zealand Loves Cycling

In New Zealand, cycling offers great Kiwi experiences such as traveling through time to gold mining days, visiting famous movie locations, and diving into a thermal pool. It is a popular sport, with many quiet roads, forest trails, and cycling tracks, with easy riding for the less experienced.

"Love 'em or hate 'em, bikes are here to stay", New Zealanders say. From the law graduate running a cargo bike delivery company to the velodrome track racer, the cycling culture is spreading all around. In addition to the commuter and the bike tourist, some other people have cycled lately:

The e-biker:
Some people, particularly those who are older or suffer from some diseases, have purchased an electric bike which gives them a power boost on hills, is fast, offers no parking problems, and is easy to get around on.

The cargo bike courier:
They can deliver packages weighing up to 80 kilos. The bike's easy to maneuver and a "green" way to get goods from A to B. Biking in the winter? No problem: wear a waterproof jacket and keep moving to stave off the cold!

The trendy campaigner:
Riding a vintage-style bike can be a great way of drawing people's attention, especially adults, to get into cycling. According to these bike riders, the main barrier to adult cycling is not cycling itself but changing their habits. They believe people need to make changes to their lives in order to make cycling work.

1 Read and listen to the information. Then answer the questions.

a Which experiences does cycling offer in New Zealand?
_____
_____

b What are the advantages of an e-bike?
_____
_____

c List the advantages of the cargo bike.
_____
_____

d What is the objective of the trendy campaigner?
_____
_____

2 Is riding bikes popular in your city? Where do people cycle?
_____
_____

3 Do you have a bike? How often do you cycle?
_____
_____

VOCABULARY 2

Endangered Animals

1 Look at pictures 1-10 on page 135 and match them with the words in the box below.

dolphin ☐	polar bear ☐
elephant ☐	rhinoceros ☐
leopard ☐	snake ☐
orangutan ☐	tiger ☐
panda ☐	turtle ☐

2 Listen and repeat.

🔊 67

3 Complete the sentences with words from activity 1.

Why are all these animals in danger of extinction?

a The _____ is a mammal. It lives in the Arctic, but the ice is disappearing.

b The _____ is a very intelligent marine mammal. It lives in the sea but thousands die in fishing nets every year.

c The _____ is the world's largest cat, but there are about 4,500 of them in the world.

d The _____ is the second biggest land mammal after the elephant. Humans hunt them for their horns.

e The _____ lives in trees in the forest, and we're destroying their habitat.

f Many species of sea _____ are hunted for their meat, eggs, skin, and shells and are now endangered.

4 Complete the chart with the words from activity 1. Can you add more animals to each habitat?

forest	savannah
orangutan	

water	other

READING 2

1 Look up the meaning of the words in the box.

| adopt   hunt   ivory   rain forest   territory |

2 Read and listen to the social environmental ad on page 135. Why do these animals need to be adopted?

🔊 68

_____
_____

3 Read the social environmental ad again. Then write T for *true* or F for *false*. Correct the false sentences.

a ☐ To adopt an animal you must pay US$36 a month.
_____
_____

b ☐ People hunt the turtle and the Asian elephant for meat.
_____
_____

c ☐ The Asian elephant and the orangutan are losing their natural habitats.
_____
_____

d ☐ An elephant's tusk is made of ivory.
_____
_____

e ☐ Donations are used to fund conservation actions in zoos.
_____
_____

f ☐ The NGO works with local partners around the world.
_____
_____

g ☐ The adopter receives a certificate and a picture.
_____
_____

4 Read again: "Have you eaten turtle soup?"

a What is the purpose of this question?
☐ Invite the reader to try turtle soup.
☐ Get the reader's attention.

b Find another question in the text with the same purpose.
_____
_____

5 ✋ **CLASS VOTE** Would you like to adopt a wild animal? Or do you prefer other conservation actions?

134 one hundred thirty-four

Adopt an Animal!

For just US$36 a year you can adopt an animal. All these animals are in danger of extinction, but you can adopt them and help them to survive.

Adopt a Turtle!
Have you eaten turtle soup? Some people hunt turtles for their meat and their eggs. Turtles are older than dinosaurs, but they could soon disappear if we don't act fast!

Adopt an Asian Elephant!
African elephants are the largest land animals, but their Asian cousins are in danger of extinction. Their natural habitat is getting smaller because we – humans – are moving into their territory. People also hunt these animals for their tusks, which are made of ivory.

Adopt an Orangutan!
Have you ever wanted an unusual pet? Did you know that people hunt orangutans for pets? They also hunt them for meat. However, the greatest danger to orangutans is the destruction of their rain forest habitat.

Where do your donations go?

We send 100% of donations to partner organizations in different countries. Your donation will fund conservation actions in the habitat of the animal you choose. We empower local communities to preserve wildlife and oppose hunting and other threats. Learn about our work at: www.friendsofwildlife.com.

You'll receive:
- ✓ a certificate of adoption
- ✓ a printed picture of your adopted animal

Friends of Wildlife

GRAMMAR 2

Present Perfect (Questions and Short Answers)

1 Complete the questions and short answers in the chart below. Use *have / haven't / has / hasn't*.

questions and short answers
_____ I / you eaten turtle soup?   Yes, I / you _____.   No, I / you _____.
_____ he / she / (it) adopted an unusual animal?   Yes, he / she / (it) _____.   No, he / she / (it) _____.
_____ we / you / they hunted elephants?   Yes, we / you / they _____.   No, we / you / they _____.

2 Order the words to make questions.

a you / Europe / Have / been / to ?
_____
_____

b abroad / worked / your dad / Has ?
_____
_____

c present / you / bought / an unusual / Have / your parents ?
_____
_____

d adopted / a / you / Have / recently / pet ?
_____
_____

3 **INTERFACE** Work in pairs. Ask a classmate the questions in activity 2. He or she is supposed to give you short answers.

➡ **GRAMMAR GUIDE** page 138

CLIL
HISTORY

1 Read and listen. When did Nelson Mandela win the Nobel Peace Prize?
_____

2 Nelson Mandela had many names. Read the box and guess which of the names all South African people called him.

Rolihlahla:	birth name given by his father
Nelson:	English name given by his school teacher
Madiba:	family "clan" name
Dalibhunga:	name given when he was 16
Tata:	nickname, this means "father" in Mandela's language, Xhosa
Khulu:	nickname, this means "grandfather" in Xhosa

_____

Apartheid

From 1948 to 1991, South Africa had a policy of legal racial discrimination called apartheid. From the Afrikaans word meaning "separation," this law enforced racial, social, and economic segregation on the native people of South Africa. When the National Party won the general election in 1948, the government passed many laws that gave white people dominance over other races. The non-white population of South Africa became second-class citizens.

Over the years there was a lot of national and international resistance to these laws, and a key person was Nelson Mandela, a native South African.

In 1964, he was sentenced to life imprisonment for his opposition to apartheid. He was released on February 11, 1990.

On April 27, 1994, South Africa celebrated its first democratic elections, and Mandela became the country's first black president. He won the Nobel Peace Prize in 1993 and, today, even after his death in 2013, he remains a symbol of freedom and equality in the world, inspiring many generations to come.

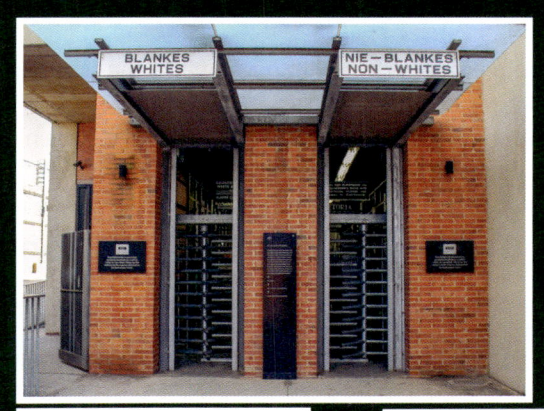

Black citizens were forbidden from using the same facilities as white (or "European") people

Nelson Mandela

3 Complete the text about Nelson Mandela with the correct dates in the box.

> 2013   1918   1994   1964

Nelson Mandela was born in **a** _____ in the village of Mvezo, in South Africa. As a young man, he became a lawyer and a political activist. He fought against apartheid. In **b** _____ he was put in prison, where he spent 26 years. He was released in 1990. Four years later, in **c** _____, he became the first black president of South Africa. He left this position in 1999, but he was still politically active for many years. He died in **d** _____.

GRAMMAR GUIDE

Present Perfect (Affirmative and Negative)

affirmative	
I've (have)	
You've (have)	
He / She / It's (has)	bought local food.
We've (have)	
You've (have)	
They've (have)	

negative	
I haven't (have not)	
You haven't (have not)	
He / She / It hasn't (has not)	used plastic bags.
We haven't (have not)	
You haven't (have not)	
They haven't (have not)	

- we use the present perfect to talk about experiences or actions in the past when we don't mention (or we don't know) the exact time of them
  I **have organized** a competition.
- we also use the present perfect to talk about past events that have an effect or a reflection in the present
  She **has painted** the house.
- we form the affirmative of the present perfect with *have / has* + the past participle of the main verb
  He **has tried** a new organic shampoo.
- we form the negative with *haven't / hasn't* + the past participle of the main verb
  They **haven't reduced** their screen time.

Present Perfect (Questions and Short Answers)

questions			short answers affirmative	short answers negative
Have	I		Yes, I have.	No, I haven't.
Have	you		Yes, you have.	No, you haven't.
Has	he / she / it	seen a snake?	Yes, he / she / it has.	No, he / she / it hasn't.
Have	we		Yes, we have.	No, we haven't.
Have	you		Yes, you have.	No, you haven't.
Have	they		Yes, they have.	No, they haven't.

- the word order is different in questions
  You **have seen** a tiger.
  Have you **seen** a tiger?
- we don't repeat the past participle in short answers
  Have you **touched** a polar bear?
  Yes, I have. / No, I haven't.

Spelling: Past Participle Regular Verbs

- for most verbs, add *-ed*
  want → want**ed**
- for verbs that end in *-e*, add *-d*
  like → like**d**
- for verbs that end in a consonant + *y*, omit the *y* and add *-ied*
  study → stud**ied**
- for verbs that end in a stressed vowel + a consonant, double the final consonant and add *-ed*
  stop → stop**ped**

Spelling: Past Participle Irregular Verbs

➡ FOR THE IRREGULAR VERBS LIST, see page 166

PROGRESS CHECK

Name: _____
Class name / Period: _____
Teacher: _____
Date: _____

Materials and Containers

1 Find nine words in the word search.

P	A	B	A	G	C	P	M	V	J
W	O	O	L	E	A	J	E	Q	A
S	O	X	A	H	R	T	T	W	R
G	L	A	S	S	T	M	A	C	K
D	G	Y	K	R	O	O	L	A	U
U	Z	B	G	H	N	Y	D	N	L
C	A	R	D	B	O	A	R	D	K

Endangered Animals

2 Identify the animals.

a p _ _ _ _

b r _ _ _ _ _ _ _ _ _

c l _ _ _ _ _ _ _

d d _ _ _ _ _ _ _

e p _ _ _ _   b _ _ _

f o _ _ _ _ _ _ _ _ _

Present Perfect (Affirmative and Negative)

3 Complete the sentences with the present perfect form of the verbs in parentheses.

a My brother _____ (swim) with dolphins in Florida.
b I _____ (see) many elephants at a sanctuary in Thailand.
c We _____ (help) fundraising campaigns for endangered animals.
d My neighbor _____ (feed) polar bears in Alaska.

4 Rewrite the sentences from activity 3 in the negative form to indicate that they are not animal friendly.

a _____
   _____
b _____
   _____
c _____
   _____
d _____
   _____

Present Perfect (Questions and Short Answers)

5 Write complete questions. Use the present perfect.

a you / reuse / paper / this week?
   _____
b your school / recycle / old test papers?
   _____
c your local supermarket / reduce / packaging?
   _____

Grammar Buildup 7

6 Complete the dialogue with the correct form of the verbs in parentheses.

Boy　Hi. You **a** _____ (look) lost.
Ava　Yes, I am.
Boy　Can I **b** _____ (help) you?
Ava　I **c** _____ (look) for the animal sanctuary.
Boy　**d** _____ (go) straight ahead past the bank. Then **e** _____ (turn) right onto Park Street.
Ava　Park Street?
Boy　Yes. The sanctuary **f** _____ (be) on your left.
Ava　**g** _____ you _____ (be) there?
Boy　Yes, I **h** _____. It's great.
Ava　What **i** _____ you _____ (see)?
Boy　Lots of things. But you have to **j** _____ (see) the peacock!

UNIT 7

VOCABULARY IN PICTURES

Materials and Containers

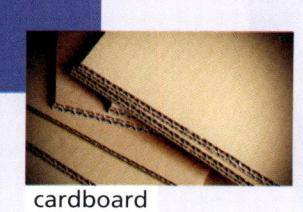

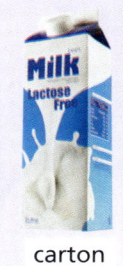

| aluminum | bag | bottle | box | can |

| cardboard | carton | cotton | glass | jar |

| metal | paper | plastic | wool |

Endangered Animals

| dolphin | elephant | leopard | orangutan | panda |

| polar bear | rhinoceros | snake | tiger | turtle |

8

ALTRUISM

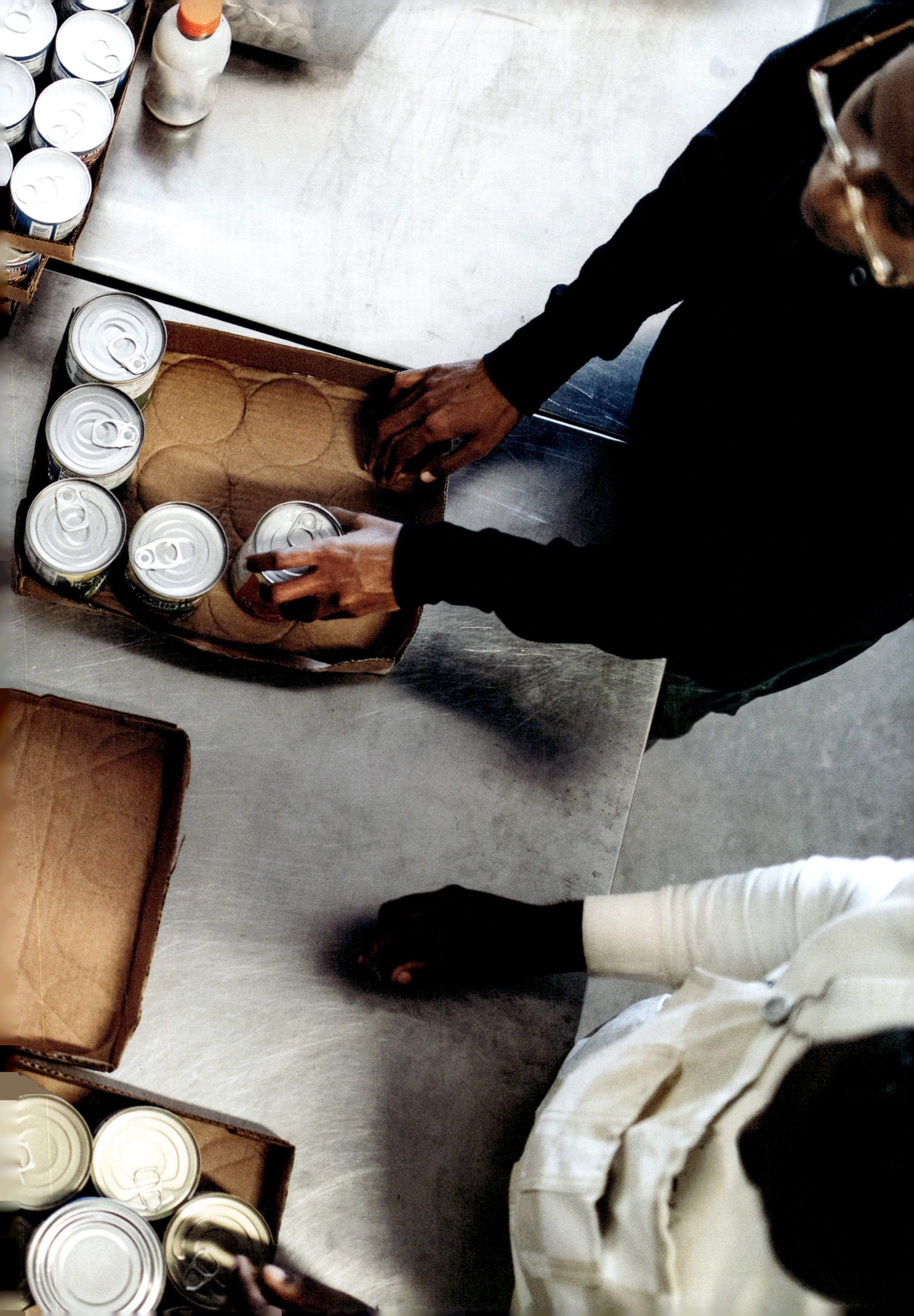

VOCABULARY 1

Fundraising Ideas

1 Match pictures 1-5 with fundraising ideas in the box.

create an online crowdfunding page ☐
donate food ☐
donate toys ☐
have a car wash day ☐
have a dog wash day ☐
have a sponsored sporting event ☐
organize a benefit concert ☐
organize a community yard sale ☐

2 Listen and repeat.

70))

3 Complete the text with words from activity 1.

After the earthquake in Haiti, lots of people from around the world wanted to help. The community donated a _____ to feed the local population. Schoolchildren donated b _____ for young kids, and they organized lots of activities in a c _____. In the USA, people created an d _____ page to raise money for the international donation campaign on the internet, and students organized e _____ to help promote the campaign too.

TIP

Sponsored sporting event can be used to refer to any sport. Use *sponsored* + the name of the sport you want refer to: *sponsored swim*, *sponsored football game*, *sponsored volleyball game*, *sponsored basketball game*, etc.

UNIT 8

📖 READING 1

1 Skim the article. Choose the best title for the text.

☐ **How to Build your Own School**   ☐ **Woman in School Fundraising Project**

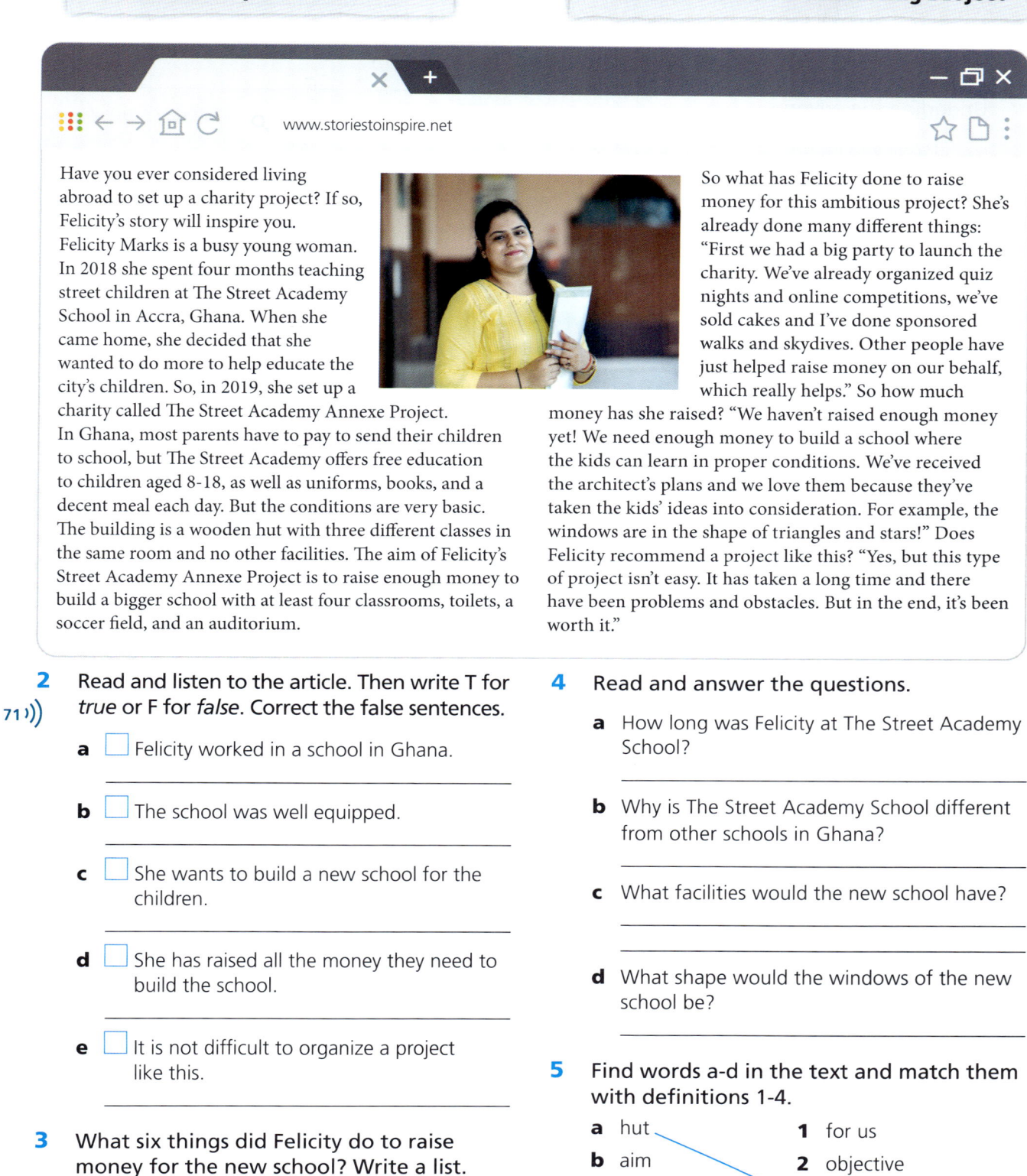

---

www.storiestoinspire.net

Have you ever considered living abroad to set up a charity project? If so, Felicity's story will inspire you. Felicity Marks is a busy young woman. In 2018 she spent four months teaching street children at The Street Academy School in Accra, Ghana. When she came home, she decided that she wanted to do more to help educate the city's children. So, in 2019, she set up a charity called The Street Academy Annexe Project. In Ghana, most parents have to pay to send their children to school, but The Street Academy offers free education to children aged 8-18, as well as uniforms, books, and a decent meal each day. But the conditions are very basic. The building is a wooden hut with three different classes in the same room and no other facilities. The aim of Felicity's Street Academy Annexe Project is to raise enough money to build a bigger school with at least four classrooms, toilets, a soccer field, and an auditorium.

So what has Felicity done to raise money for this ambitious project? She's already done many different things: "First we had a big party to launch the charity. We've already organized quiz nights and online competitions, we've sold cakes and I've done sponsored walks and skydives. Other people have just helped raise money on our behalf, which really helps." So how much money has she raised? "We haven't raised enough money yet! We need enough money to build a school where the kids can learn in proper conditions. We've received the architect's plans and we love them because they've taken the kids' ideas into consideration. For example, the windows are in the shape of triangles and stars!" Does Felicity recommend a project like this? "Yes, but this type of project isn't easy. It has taken a long time and there have been problems and obstacles. But in the end, it's been worth it."

---

2 🔊 71 Read and listen to the article. Then write T for *true* or F for *false*. Correct the false sentences.

a ☐ Felicity worked in a school in Ghana.
_____

b ☐ The school was well equipped.
_____

c ☐ She wants to build a new school for the children.
_____

d ☐ She has raised all the money they need to build the school.
_____

e ☐ It is not difficult to organize a project like this.
_____

3 What six things did Felicity do to raise money for the new school? Write a list.
_____
_____
_____
_____

4 Read and answer the questions.

a How long was Felicity at The Street Academy School?
_____

b Why is The Street Academy School different from other schools in Ghana?
_____

c What facilities would the new school have?
_____

d What shape would the windows of the new school be?
_____

5 Find words a-d in the text and match them with definitions 1-4.

a hut — 1 for us
b aim   2 objective
c launch 3 a small, simple building
d on our behalf 4 initiate (a product or project)

one hundred forty-five **145**

GRAMMAR 1

Present Perfect: *ever, never, yet, already, just*

1 Read the sentences below. Write A in case of affirmative sentences, B in case of negative sentences, and C for questions. <u>Underline</u> the adverbs.

a ☐ Have you ever done a sponsored swim?

b ☐ My sister has already donated all of her toys.

c ☐ I've never given any money to charity organizations.

d ☐ We haven't organized the food donations yet.

e ☐ The sponsored football game has just started.

2 Complete the rules with *ever, never, already, yet,* or *just*. Then complete the chart with these words.

The words *ever*, *never*, *already*, *yet*, and *just* are often used with the present perfect.

a _____ is used to talk about something which is expected to happen. It means "at any time up to now." It is used in questions and negative sentences and placed at the end of them.

b _____ is used to express a negative idea.

c _____ is usually used with the present perfect tense and means "a short time ago." It comes before the main verb.

d We often use _____ to ask if something has happened at any time before now.

e _____ is used to say that something has happened early. It usually comes before the main verb.

	present perfect with *ever, never, yet, already, just*
+	Felicity has _____ done lots of things for the project. I have _____ finished helping Felicity.
−	The charity hasn't raised enough money for the new building _____. My friend Jill has _____ taken part in a sponsored volleyball game. She'll play next time.
?	Have you _____ been to Ghana? Have the kids donated any toys _____?

3 Write complete sentences in the present perfect affirmative, negative, or interrogative form. Note where to insert the adverbs.

a I / do / a sponsored swim / yet ✗
_____

b My friends / organized / lots of barbecues / already ✓
_____

c Mark / organize / a car wash day / just ✓
_____

d you / organize / a dog wash day / ever ?
_____

e My mom / raise / so much money / for charity / never ✗
_____

f Maggie / donate / the toys / for charity / yet ?
_____

4 Complete the text with the present perfect form of the verbs in parentheses and the adverbs provided.

To: Barbara
From: Petra
Subject: Raising money for charity

Hi, Barbara,
a _____ you _____ (ever / raise) money for charity? I
b _____ (not do) anything before, but I really want to be a volunteer. My brother
c _____ (just / finish) creating an online crowdfunding page to raise money for cancer research and he d _____ (already / help) as a volunteer in charity organizations. My sisters e _____ (organize) a dog wash day at our school to raise money for the Red Cross. I
f _____ to the Red Cross _____ (not donate / yet)! I want to do a sponsored swim because I think it is a good way to raise money. My brother and sisters g _____ any money for an animal charity _____ (not raise / yet), so I want to raise money for the ASPCA. Do you think that's a good idea? Oh, God, I h _____ (never be) so happy! Will you help me organize the sponsored swim?

Petra

UNIT 8

PRONUNCIATION
Contractions

Listen and repeat the sentences.

72 🔊 a I've done a sponsored swim.
    b You haven't finished your homework.
    c She hasn't got a badge.
    d He's raised over $1,000.

5 Choose the correct options.

Gina Have you **a ever / never** ridden a horse, Colin?
Colin No, I **b have / haven't**. **c Have / Had** you?
Gina No, I haven't. I've **d ever / never** done anything interesting.
Colin I don't believe you. Everyone's **e done / doing** something interesting.
Gina I **f haven't / hasn't**.
Colin OK, have you ever **g meet / met** a famous person?
Gina No. Have **h you / she**?
Colin Erm … yes. I know, **i have you / you have** ever eaten Indian food?
Gina No, I've **j ever / never** eaten it.
Colin Have you ever **k been / being** in a movie?
Gina You mean as an actor?
Colin Yes. Well, **l had / have** you?
Gina Yes, I **m have / did**. But years ago. I've **n forgotten / forgetted** all about it.

6 Listen and check your answers.
73 🔊

➡ **GRAMMAR GUIDE** page 154

🎧 LISTENING

Charity Appeals

1 Work in pairs. Write a list of famous charities and what they do.

2 Listen to the radio program. Which charities do the speakers mention?
74 🔊
a The Red Cross
b Oxfam
c The Red Crescent
d Médecins Sans Frontières
e Comic Relief
f ASPCA

3 Listen again and choose the correct options.
74 🔊
a Oxfam helps **animals / hungry people / sick people**.
b MSF helps **animals / hungry people / sick people**.
c The ASPCA helps **animals / hungry people / sick people**.

4 Listen again. Then write T for *true* or F for *false*. Correct the false sentences.
74 🔊
a ☐ Oxfam wants people to give money for their stores.
_____
_____

b ☐ Oxfam has 15,000 stores worldwide.
_____
_____

c ☐ A group of Spanish doctors started MSF.
_____
_____

d ☐ MSF needs people to volunteer for them.
_____
_____

e ☐ The ASPCA looks after animals all over the world.
_____
_____

f ☐ The ASPCA gets money from donations.
_____
_____

5 👥 **INTERFACE** Work in pairs. Reflect about the importance and contribution of the charity institutions from activity 2.

> I think Oxfam is important because it helps people who are hungry in emergency situations.

SPEAKING

An Audio Ad about a Fundraising Event

1 Read and listen to the audio ad script. What event is being advertised?

🔊 75

AUDIO AD SCRIPT	
SOUND EFFECTS	School noises. The break signal rings and students go out into the hallway to talk.
GIRL 1	Are you going to Megan's party, Maddie?
GIRL 2	Sure! Too bad I don't have the money to buy a new pair of shoes.
GIRL 1	Oh, but there's a community yard sale going on at Zoe's house. There's a lot of cool stuff, and it's all very cheap! What's more, all the profit goes to the local church homeless program.
GIRL 2	Wow! It's my chance to buy some shoes at a nice price … and still do good!
MALE ANNOUNCER VOICE	Zoe's Community Yard Sale. Every Sunday in May, from 9am to 8pm, at 30 Orchard Street. Get a good deal and help your community!

TIP

Audio ads run on the radio, podcasts, and music streaming apps. They typically last 30 seconds and try to persuade the listener to do something, like buy a product or contribute to a cause. Many ads end with a **call to action** – a statement that encourages the audience to do something. An audio ad is usually based on a written script.

2 Check (✓) the correct information.

  a The words in bold on the left …
  ☐ are read by the announcers.
  ☐ give directions on how to record the ad.

  b The ad appeals to …
  ☐ young people.
  ☐ people over 50.

  c The male voice at the end serves to …
  ☐ make fun of the characters' dialogue.
  ☐ highlight the final message.

3 Circle the sentence in the script that talks about a problem many listeners may have.

4 Underline the passage that presents the event as a solution to this problem.

5 Locate one **call to action** in the script.

FUNCTIONAL LANGUAGE

Advertising a Charity Event
All the profit goes to …
Do good!
Help your community!

Speaking Task

Step 1

Work in small groups. Choose a fundraising event:

A community yard sale   A garage sale   A bric-a-brac sale

Step 2

Create an audio ad encouraging the community to join the event. Plan a dialogue-based script. Follow these tips:

- Make listeners identify with the message. Talk about a problem they probably have (e.g., not having money to buy things) and show the event as a solution to the problem.
- End the script with a call to action. Use imperative (*come, do, help*).
- In addition to the characters, you can use a third voice to highlight key points.
- Consider using music or sound effects.

Step 3

Act out the script considering it goes for about 30 seconds. If necessary, make adjustments and record a final version. Then present the ad to the class.

UNIT 8

🌐 CULTURE

Good Deeds Day in India

Good Deeds Day is a global celebration which unites people from over 100 countries to do good deeds for the benefit of others and the planet: every single person can do something good to improve the lives of others and, therefore, help change the world for the better.

In addition to changing some groups' attitudes during Good Deeds Day, the Non-Violence Project Foundation (NVP) in India wants to inspire, engage, and motivate young people to understand how to solve conflicts peacefully. They focus on two areas: Education and Raising Awareness. They believe in education and follow Mahatma Gandhi's words: "If you want to change the world, you must start with the children." Inspiring youth through education is their philosophy. They understand education has the power to build and ensure a strong base for tolerance, acceptance, and respect for human rights.

Their approach is based on interaction and creativity and they count on teachers, sport coaches, and youth leaders to interact with young people face-to-face, or through e-learning.

Good Deeds Day is, then, a great opportunity to share such good deeds with the world!

Indian school children looking outside the window from their classroom, Rajasthan, India

1 Read and listen to the information. Then match the two parts to make sentences. (76)

a Good Deeds Day seeks to call people's attention to the importance …
b The NVP in India wishes to inspire and motivate …
c Their philosophy is …
d Education, in the NVP's view, has the power …
e They count on teachers, sport coaches, and youth leaders to interact …

☐ … "inspiring through education."
☐ … of doing something good to improve the lives of others.
☐ … with young people face-to-face or through e-learning.
☐ … young people to understand how to solve conflicts without using violence.
☐ … to build tolerance, acceptance, and respect for everyone.

2 Is Good Deeds Day celebrated in your country? What do people do on this day?
_____
_____
_____
_____

3 Have you done any good deed recently? Read some good deed ideas. Check (✓) the ones you have done. Share your answers with your classmates.

a ☐ Help a friend in need.
b ☐ Volunteer for an hour at an organization of your choice.
c ☐ Write a thank-you note to someone who won't expect it.
d ☐ Find unneeded items in your house and donate them to a charitable organization.
e ☐ Plant a tree.
f ☐ Think of something you do well, and use your talent to benefit others – for example, perform magic tricks at a children's hospital.
g ☐ Teach an elderly person to use a computer to surf the net.
h ☐ Collect stuffed animals or toys from family members, friends, and neighbors and donate them to an organization that helps children.
i ☐ Donate supplies to children from underprivileged homes.

VOCABULARY 2

make and do

1 Do we use *make* or *do* with the phrases in the box? Write the correct answers.

_____ a decision	_____ money
_____ a mistake	_____ nothing
_____ charity work	_____ someone a favor
_____ exercise	_____ someone happy
_____ friends	_____ someone laugh
_____ homework	_____ your best

2 Listen, check your answers, and repeat.

3 Match pictures a-e with phrases from activity 1.

a _____

b _____

c _____

d _____

e _____

4 Complete the questions with the correct form of *make* or *do*.

Have you ever _____*done*_____ any charity work?

a What _____ you happy?
b Which people _____ you laugh?
c What's the biggest mistake you have ever _____?
d How often do you _____ someone a favor?
e How often do you _____ exercise?
f What's the most difficult decision you have ever _____?
g Where do you usually _____ your homework?
h What's the best way to _____ a lot of money?

5 **INTERFACE** Work in pairs. Ask and answer the questions in activity 4.

Have you ever done any charity work?

Yes, me and my classmates organized a benefit concert in my school.

READING 2

1 Look at the pictures of Selena Gomez on page 151 and answer the questions.

a Have you ever heard of Selena Gomez?
b What do you know about her?

2 Skim the personal profile on page 151. Why is Selena Gomez famous?

_____

SELENA GOMEZ, GOODWILL AMBASSADOR

Selena Gomez has been famous for over 15 years. She's an American actor, singer, producer, and more recently she founded Rare Beauty, a makeup company.

In 2008, she starred in a hit TV series, and her band, Selena Gomez and the Scene, released a hit album. Since then, Selena has been focused on every aspect of her career. She's a busy girl!

But Selena still finds time to do lots of charity work too. She supports Island Dog, a charity that helps dogs in Puerto Rico, and Raise Hope for Congo, a charity that campaigns against violence towards Congolese women.

Since August 2009, Selena has been a UNICEF Goodwill Ambassador. She has been to Ghana to visit children who are living without enough food or clean water. She realized that she was publicizing their problems by visiting Ghana. This is what being a Goodwill Ambassador is all about – making people aware of the world's problems and encouraging them to help.

Selena working as an ambassador for UNICEF.

Selena at a Raise Hope for the Congo event, in Hollywood.

Selena loves animals and supports a charity that helps dogs.

4 Have a look at these other UNICEF Goodwill Ambassadors. Then discuss the questions with a classmate and share your thoughts with the class.

Argentinian soccer player Lionel Messi

Colombian singer Shakira

American actor Whoopi Goldberg

Hong Kong actor Jackie Chan

a Why is it important for a Goodwill Ambassador to be a famous person?

b Besides fame, what else do you think a UNICEF Goodwill Ambassador needs to have?

3 Read and listen to the personal profile. Then answer the questions.

78

a How long has Selena been famous?
_____

b What charities does she work for?
_____

c When did she become a UNICEF Goodwill Ambassador?
_____

d Why did she visit Ghana for UNICEF?
_____
_____

e Why are Goodwill Ambassadors important?
_____
_____

5 **INTERFACE** Keep working in pairs. Do Goodwill Ambassadors do an important job?

> Yes, because they publicize problems around the world.

> No. They give the public the feeling that something is being done for the poor, but it's all marketing.

GRAMMAR 2

Present Perfect: *for* and *since*

1. Read the sentences below. Underline the verbs in the present perfect and circle the time expressions.

   a Selena Gomez has been famous for over 15 years.
   b Selena has been a UNICEF Goodwill Ambassador since August 2009.
   c Her fans have loved her since she started singing.
   d Selena has worked as an actor for some time now.
   e How long has she supported Island Dog?

2. Look at the sentences in activity 1 again and complete the rules with *for*, *how long*, or *since*.

   a We often use a clause with _____ to show when something started in the past.
   b We often use a clause with _____ to indicate periods of time.
   c _____ is used in questions to ask about the duration of an activity.

3. Complete the chart with *for*, *how long*, and *since*.

Present perfect with *for* and *since*
_____ has she been a Goodwill Ambassador?
She has been an ambassador _____ 2009.
She has been an ambassador _____ over ten years.

4. Complete the chart with the time expressions in the box.

   | 2020 2pm a long time a month |
   | April I was born last night Saturday |
   | this morning three weeks two hours |

since	for

5. Complete the text using *for* or *since*.

   My hero is my grandfather. He's 80 years old. He loves soccer and he has watched every Arsenal game a _____ 1951. He hasn't missed a game b _____ the day he got married – it was a Saturday. He's been married c _____ over 60 years and he and my grandma have lived with us d _____ five years. He loves music and he's been a fan of hip-hop e _____ 2011 when I played him one of my favorite hip-hop songs. He's the coolest grandfather in the world.

6. Write questions with *How long*.

   you / be / at this school
   How long have you been at this school?

   a he / know / his best friend
   _____
   b you / study / English
   _____
   c you / have / your cell phone
   _____
   d you / live / in your apartment
   _____
   e they / have / their dog
   _____

➡ **GRAMMAR GUIDE** page 154

WRITING

A Newsletter Article

1 EXPLORING THE CONTEXT

1. Skim the article on page 153. What is the name of the school the students in the headline attend?

   TIP

   A newsletter is a printed or electronic publication produced by a business or an organization. It contains updates and announcements and is sent to people connected to the organization. For example, a school might distribute a newsletter to students, parents, and teachers.

2. Read and listen. What have the students done to raise money for charity?

UNIT 8

St. Anne School NEWSLETTER

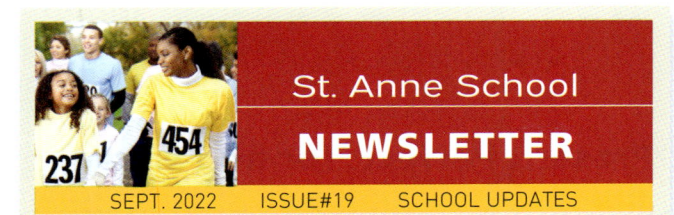

SEPT. 2022 · ISSUE#19 · SCHOOL UPDATES

10th grade students raise over $1,500 for the ASPCA

On the last Sunday of August, the 28th, our 10th grade class did a sponsored walk to help the ASPCA. Students are celebrating the success of the event.

Rachel Jones, the math teacher who organized the walk, said, "We wanted to do something to help animals because many of us have pets and we are all animal lovers. We all enjoy walking, so we decided to do a sponsored walk at the local park." Over 200 parents and friends were at the park to support the students. More than 300 people have promised sponsorship money, so the total will probably be more than $2,000 when the students have collected all the money.

Principal Sean Kemp is very proud of the students. "We've never done a sponsored walk before. I hope it will become an annual event because it has been such a success."

3 A news article must answer to the so-called *5 Ws + 1 H*. Find them in the text and complete.

- **W**hat? raised over $1,500
- a **W**ho? _____
- b **W**hen? _____
- c **W**here? _____
- d **W**hy? _____
- e **H**ow? _____

4 Which people were interviewed for the article?
_____

5 In your opinion, who else could be interviewed?
_____

2 PLANNING

1. Join a classmate and write an article (120-150 words) about a recent local event.
2. Gather information and write down the *5 Ws + 1 H* of the event: **W**hat happened? **W**ho was involved? **W**here? **W**hen? **W**hy? **H**ow?
3. Think of two people you could interview for the article.

4. Ask them two or three objective questions about the event. Record their answers because later you will transcribe them in the text.

LANGUAGE FOCUS

so and because

We all enjoy walking, **so** we decided to do a sponsored walk.
We wanted to do something to help animals **because** many of us have pets.

1 Look at the sentences above and complete the rules with the words *so* and *because*.
- a We use _____ to show the result.
- b We use _____ to give a reason.

2 Join the sentences with *because* or *so*.
- a The art teacher organized an exhibition. There were many beautiful paintings by the students.
_____
_____
- b Students wanted to raise money. They sold raffle tickets.
_____
_____

3 WRITING

1. Write a first draft. Use your notes from Step 2 and the St. Anne School's newsletter.
2. Include a quote from each interviewee. Don't forget the quotation marks.

4 CHECKING & EDITING

1. Ask another pair to read your draft and check:
   - Are the *5 Ws + 1 H* answered?
   - Is the punctuation correct?
   - Is the headline informative?
   - Was a picture of the event included?
2. Use your classmates' suggestions to prepare the final version of your article.

5 SHARING

1. Submit your articles to the school's newsletter.
2. If your school does not have a newsletter, you can create one. There are already enough articles for the first edition!

GRAMMAR GUIDE

Present Perfect: *ever, never, yet, already, just*

Have you **ever** lived in France?
I have **never** lived in France.
Have you lived in France **yet**?
I haven't lived in France **yet**.
I have **already** lived in France.
The sponsored swim has **just** started.

- we often use the adverb *ever* to ask if something has happened at any time before now
- we use *never* to express a negative idea
- we use *already* to say that something has happened early. It usually comes before the main verb
- we use *yet* to talk about something which is expected to happen. It means "at any time up to now." It is used in questions and negative sentences and placed at the end of them
- we usually use *just* with the present perfect tense, and it means "a short time ago." It comes before the main verb

Present Perfect: *for* and *since*

How long has she been a Goodwill Ambassador?
She's been an ambassador **since** August 2009.
She's been an ambassador **for** more than a year.

for (a period in time)	since (a point in time)
ten minutes	2020
two hours	2pm
four days	April
three weeks	this morning
a month	I was born
a year	Saturday
a long time	last night

- we use *How long* with present perfect questions to ask about the duration of an activity or situation
  How long has she been a doctor?
- we use *for* with durations of time
  She's been a doctor **for more than a year**.
- we use *since* with starting points in time (when the activity commenced)
  She's been a doctor **since August 2009**.

PROGRESS CHECK

Name: _____
Class name / Period: _____
Teacher: _____
Date: _____

Fundraising Ideas

1 Match a-f with 1-6 to make sentences.

a ☐ Dan and Rita are donating
b ☐ My car is a bit dirty so I'm going
c ☐ Pop stars are making a
d ☐ My friends are creating
e ☐ A woman from a children's charity project is collecting
f ☐ Our dogs have been in the mud

1 toys for kids.
2 charity benefit concert to raise money.
3 food to a local charity.
4 to that car wash day for charity.
5 so I'm going to that dog wash day at the school.
6 an international online crowdfunding page for victims of the earthquake.

make and do

2 Complete the sentences with the correct form of make or do.

a I've just _____ some exercise. I'm really tired.
b I always _____ my homework before I watch TV.
c Ken is so funny. He really _____ me laugh.
d Can you _____ me a favor? I really need some help.
e Robin wants to _____ some charity work in Africa for a year.
f I think I failed the test. I _____ too many mistakes.

Present Perfect: ever, never, yet, already, just

3 Complete the sentences with ever, never, yet, already, or just.

a Beth has _____ done a sponsored swim.
b My brother has _____ met some people.
c Have you _____ raised money for charity?
d I haven't visited India _____, but I want to.
e Have you seen the new adventure movie _____?
f Alex has _____ collected lots of money for charity.

Present Perfect: for and since

4 Complete the sentences with for or since.

a Tom's been here _____ a long time. He arrived early.
b Carla's done charity work _____ she was 12.
c Selena Gomez has been famous _____ many years.
d You've studied _____ three hours. Well done!
e I haven't eaten _____ this morning. I'm hungry.
f I've known my best friend _____ 2019.

Grammar Buildup 8

5 Choose the correct answers.

a _____ you know someone you really admire? I do. My best friend, Mike. We've known each other since we b _____ primary school and we've been best friends c _____ five years. Mike loves d _____ other people. He e _____ lots of money for charity.

He's washed cars and he plays trumpet, so he f _____ a benefit concert at our school, and he always supports other fundraising ideas. I've done some events with him. For example, we've held a sponsored volleyball game to raise money for the ASPCA.

We think ASPCA is the g _____ important charity in the world. The only thing Mike has h _____ done is a sponsored walk, but he's going to do one this summer. He's fantastic!

a	Do	Have
b	start	started
c	for	since
d	help	helping
e	is raising	has raised
f	organize	organized
g	more	most
h	never	ever

UNIT 8

VOCABULARY IN PICTURES

Fundraising Ideas

- create an online crowdfunding page
- donate food 
- donate toys 
- have a car wash day 
- have a dog wash day 
- have a sponsored sporting event 
- organize a benefit concert 
- organize a community yard sale 

make and do

- make a decision
- make a mistake 
- make friends 
- make money 
- make someone happy 
- make someone laugh 
- do charity work 
- do exercise 
- do homework 
- do nothing 
- do someone a favor 
- do your best

REVIEW 4

VOCABULARY

Start

1. Have you ever donate _____ for charity?

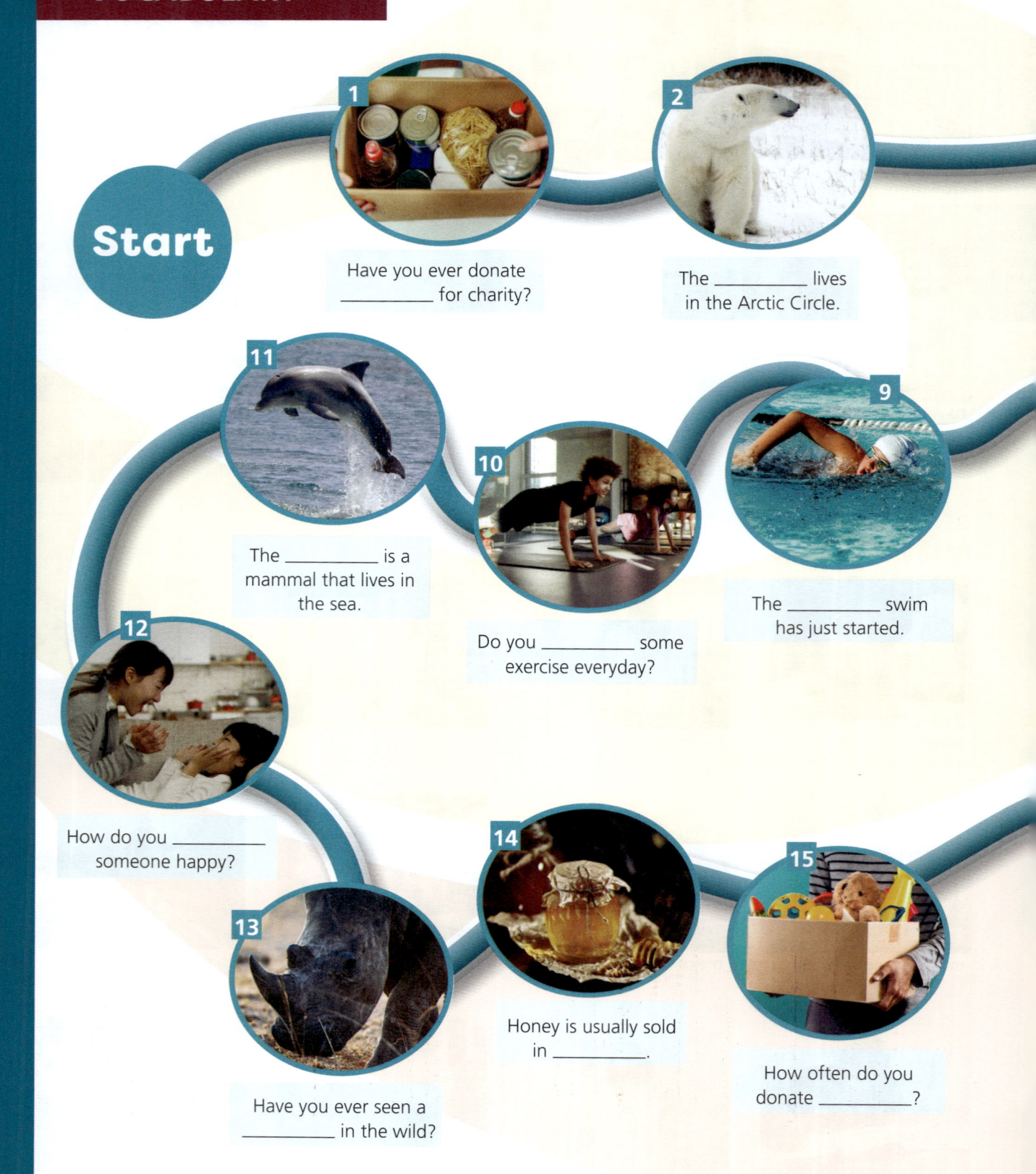

2. The _____ lives in the Arctic Circle.

11. The _____ is a mammal that lives in the sea.

10. Do you _____ some exercise everyday?

9. The _____ swim has just started.

12. How do you _____ someone happy?

13. Have you ever seen a _____ in the wild?

14. Honey is usually sold in _____.

15. How often do you donate _____?

3 What _____ you laugh?

4 This cake takes a whole _____ of milk.

5 The _____ is the biggest land animal.

6 When I'm tired, I like _____ nothing.

7 Have you ever bought something at a _____ ?

8 _____ is made from wood.

16 Sweaters, gloves, and scarves are often made of _____.

17 Do you always _____ your homework?

18 You should recycle your used _____.

Finish

REVIEW 4

GRAMMAR

Present Perfect (Affirmative and Negative)

1 Write the past participle form of the regular and irregular verbs.

organize _organized_ **e** have _____
see _seen_ **f** choose _____
a stop _____ **g** read _____
b play _____ **h** become _____
c try _____ **i** do _____
d open _____ **j** make _____

2 Complete the sentences with *have* or *has* and the past participle form of one of the verbs in the box.

~~build~~ buy do have make see

They ___have built___ the new library.

a I _____ a mistake.
b Gemma _____ a new bag.
c The students _____ voluntary work.
d I _____ my hair cut this month.
e My brother _____ the Tower of London.

3 Write sentences in the present perfect affirmative form.

I / read / a great book
I have read a great book.

a my sister / promise / to take me to the benefit concert
b my uncle and aunt / open / a new hotel
c I / meet / several famous people
d we / have / fish for lunch
e they / arrive / early for the game
f you / become / very brave

4 Rewrite the sentences in the negative form.

I've seen this movie five times.
I haven't seen this movie five times.

a My uncle has sailed around the world alone.
b I have finished this activity.
c My friend Dan has bought my old laptop.
d At school, we have reduced our waste.

Present Perfect (Questions and Short Answers)

5 Look at Kate's to-do list. Write questions and short answers using the present perfect affirmative and negative form.

a	recycle plastic bottles …	✓
b	turn off the TV …	✗
c	throw away clothes …	✗
d	buy local food …	✓
e	become vegetarian …	✓

a _____
b _____
c _____
d _____
e _____

160 one hundred sixty

Present Perfect: *ever, never, yet, already, just*

6 Complete the sentences using the present perfect form of the verbs in parentheses. Add *already* or *just*, according to the clues given.

They __have already built__ (build) the new hospital. (It was ready earlier than expected.)

a My dad _____ (break) his leg. (He can't walk right now.)

b She _____ (have) lunch. (She doesn't need to eat for at least three hours.)

c We _____ (create) an online crowdfunding page. (We have been through this experience before.)

d Louie _____ (post) a new picture. (The Facebook status says "just now.")

7 Complete these sentences with *ever* and *never*.

I've __never__ played the trumpet.

a Have you _____ swum in a lake?

b My boyfriend has _____ driven a car.

c Have your friends _____ played rugby?

d She's ridden a bike, but she's _____ ridden a motorcycle.

8 Write questions in the present perfect form.

you / ever / meet / a scientist ?
Have you ever met a scientist?

a your parents / sell / yet / their house ?
_____

b Miss Martinez / ever / give / you a bad grade ?
_____

c you / ever / eat / fish ?
_____

d Charlie / yet / wash / his dad's car ?
_____

9 Write answers for the questions in activity 8.

[X] No, I have never met a scientist.

a [✓] _____

b [X] _____

c [✓] _____

d [✓] _____

Present Perfect: *for* and *since*

10 Complete the chart with the time expressions in the box.

> a few minutes   a long time   a year
> eight months   February
> hours   last year
> 9 o'clock   ~~2019~~

for	since
_____	2019
_____	_____
_____	_____
_____	_____
_____	_____

11 Complete the sentences with *for* or *since*.

My dad hasn't worked __for__ ten years.

a "How long has there been a cathedral here? _____ more than five centuries."

b We've known each other _____ last summer.

c Henry has wanted to be an actor _____ he was young.

d They haven't seen Katy _____ two weeks.

e Tuvalu has been an independent country _____ 1978.

f Europeans have inhabited this island _____ over 400 years.

DIGITAL LITERACY

Using and Sharing Intellectual Property

Stealing Ideas

Panel 1: This definition of renewable energy is perfect! I'll use it in my science homework.

Panel 2: Love this song! I'm going to use it on the soundtrack for my skateboarding video!

Panel 3: Later ...
I've read this text before ... You didn't write it, did you, Lily?
In fact, I found it online.

Panel 4: Hey, guys! I have uploaded the video for us to submit for the contest!
Great!

Panel 5: It's OK to use someone else's piece of writing in your paper, but you must enclose the text in quotation marks ... And you must give credit to the original author! You will have to redo this homework tonight in your own words.

Panel 6: Hey, the video was removed for violating the copyright of a rock band!
Tsk-tsk ... You should have used royalty-free music on the soundtrack.
Oh no! ...

1 Read and listen. Then match the sentences.

🔊 80

a Lily copied into her science paper
b Lily failed to give
c Daniel used
d Daniel's video was
e The teacher spotted
f Daniel should have

1 ☐ removed for copyright infringement.
2 ☐ a definition she found online.
3 ☐ used royalty-free music.
4 ☐ the proper credit to the source.
5 ☐ the plagiarism in Lily's paper.
6 ☐ a copyrighted song in his video.

2 Complete the text with the words in the box.

credit   permission   quotation marks   royalty-free

Mindful use and sharing of intellectual property includes …

- … giving _____ when you're sharing someone else's content.
- … using _____ when you're quoting the author verbatim (without changing the words).
- … knowing about and using _____ content.
- … asking for _____ when you want to use copyrighted content.

3 Work in pairs. Read the comic again and organize your ideas in the diagram below.

ACTION
What did they do?
They used someone else's intellectual work.

REASONS Why did she do it?	CONSEQUENCES What was the result of her actions?	REASONS Why did he do it?	CONSEQUENCES What was the result of his actions?

4 Discuss the following questions with a classmate. Then share your thoughts with the class. Be sincere!

a Have you ever used someone else's intellectual work, as Lily and Daniel did? What was it?
b What were your reasons? Why did you do it?
c Did your actions have consequences? If yes, which ones?

5 Now, read the quote and discuss the question below. In your notebook, write a paragraph stating your conclusion. As a class, organize an online forum and share your views.

> "Ethical behavior is doing the right thing when no one else is watching […]."
> Aldo Leopold (1887-1948), American writer

- If there were no consequences, would it be OK to use someone else's intellectual work? Why?

GLOBAL CITIZENSHIP

My Carbon Footprint

- Do you know what a carbon footprint is?
- How do our day-to-day activities contribute to the climate crisis?
- How can we have a less negative impact on the environment's health?

1 Read the text about carbon footprints. Write the headings from the box in the correct places. Then listen and confirm your answers.

> Consumption   Food   Household energy   Transportation

What is a Carbon Footprint?

All our activities contribute directly or indirectly to the emission of greenhouse gases. The carbon footprint is a method created to calculate the amount of greenhouse gases that an individual or an organization emits over a set period of time, usually a year.
Discover the four categories usually measured in a carbon footprint calculator.

a _____

If you live in a home powered by solar or wind energy, your carbon footprint will be lighter. But if your home is powered by fossil energy (coal or natural gas), your carbon footprint will be heavier. Another important thing is the use of air conditioners and electric heaters. These appliances consume a lot of energy and increase your footprint.

b _____

If you travel by bus, subway, or bicycle, you contribute less to global warming than if you used a car. Do you like to travel by plane? Unfortunately, air travel also increases your carbon footprint.

c _____

Clothes, shoes, electronics, personal items ... All this consumes water, energy, and fuel to produce and to reach you. The more you consume, the heavier your carbon footprint is.

d _____

If you consume a lot of animal source foods, your carbon footprint is heavier. The same applies if you prefer processed or imported foods.

> **TIP**
> Want to calculate your carbon footprint? There are many calculators available online. Try this one (or another one your teacher recommends): https://depts.washington.edu/i2sea/iscfc/calculate.php. Accessed on: June 3, 2022.

2 Maybe you still can't change your home energy source or the means of transport you use, but choosing more environmentally friendly foods is within your reach! In pairs, circle the food item in each food group that you think emits the most greenhouse gases.

STARCHES	PROTEINS	FRUIT & VEG
bread oatmeal pasta potatoes rice	beans beef chicken eggs farmed fish	apples avocados bananas berries & grapes tomatoes

164 one hundred sixty-four

Global Attitudes & Action

3 Read the text below and check your answers. Discuss with a classmate: Given what you know about global warming: why do you think beef production is so harmful to the environment?

> **Food and Carbon Emissions**
> Food production is responsible for a quarter of all greenhouse gas emissions.
> Among starches, rice is the most harmful to the environment because it is grown in flooded fields, which emit a lot of methane.
> In the group of fruits and vegetables, the avocado is a villain because its cultivation has been done in areas of cleared forests.
> Finally, in the group of proteins, animal products are the ones that most contribute to global warming. No less than 58% of emissions from food come from animal products. And, of that portion, half comes from beef and lamb.
> Eggs are the animal protein that emits the least greenhouse gases. Yet their production emits much more than plant-based proteins such as beans and nuts.

Food and Climate Crisis: A Self-Assessment

For a week, investigate how much your own eating habits add to your carbon footprint. Then you can define simple changes and apply them.

DOING

1 Work in groups of 4-5. For one week, each of you will complete the chart below.

How often did I do it?	🟢	🟡	🟠	🟠	🔴
a Eat red meat					
b Consume dairy					
c Throw out food					
d Eat out of season fruits and veggies					
e Have processed foods or drinks					

Key: 🟢 never 🟡 1-2x / week 🟠 3-5x / week
     🟠 1x / day 🔴 2x / day +

2 After collecting the data, discuss:

　a What are the group averages for each item? Are there any outliers?

　b Were you aware that these eating habits could increase your impact on the environment?

　c What changes could you make to eat more sustainably?

3 Implement the planned changes. Work together with your family to achieve your goals.

4 Reproduce the chart in activity 1 in your notebook to track your progress for another week. Mark the changes in frequency in a different color. Circle the items that remained unchanged.

5 Discuss as a group: How successful have you been in adopting a more sustainable diet? What were the biggest obstacles?

PRESENTING

1 Create a column chart comparing the group averages for week 1 and week 2.

2 Write a short text describing what you did, what results you expected to achieve, and what actually happened.

3 Present your chart to your classmates and share how this two-week self-assessment went.

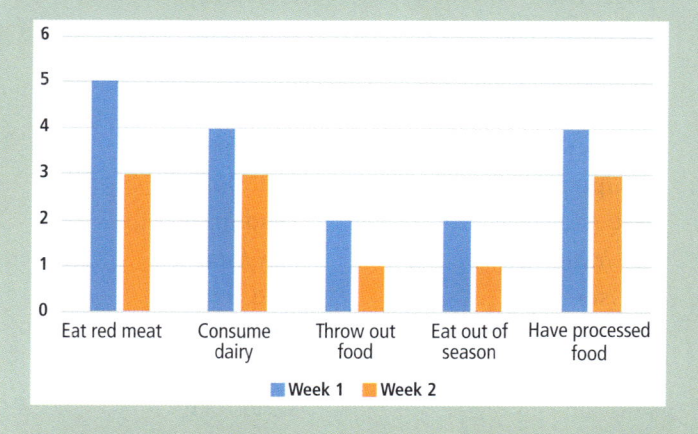

	Eat red meat	Consume dairy	Throw out food	Eat out of season	Have processed food
Week 1	5	4	2	2	4
Week 2	3	3	1	1	3

REFLECTING

Discuss as a class:

　a What did you learn from this experiment? Was your family also impacted? How?

　b Besides food, what other habits could you change to lighten your carbon footprint?

IRREGULAR VERBS

Infinitive	Simple Past	Past Participle
be /bi/	was / were /wɑz/, /wɜr/	been /bin/, /bɪn/
begin /bɪˈgɪn/	began /bɪˈgæn/	begun /bɪˈgʌn/
break /breɪk/	broke /broʊk/	broken /ˈbroʊkən/
bring /brɪŋ/	brought /brɔt/	brought /brɔt/
build /bɪld/	built /bɪlt/	built /bɪlt/
buy /baɪ/	bought /bɔt/	bought /bɔt/
choose /tʃuz/	chose /tʃoʊz/	chosen /ˈtʃoʊz(ə)n/
come /kʌm/	came /keɪm/	come /kʌm/
do /du/	did /dɪd/	done /dʌn/
drink /drɪŋk/	drank /dræŋk/	drunk /drʌŋk/
drive /draɪv/	drove /droʊv/	driven /ˈdrɪv(ə)n/
eat /it/	ate /eɪt/	eaten /ˈit(ə)n/
fall /fɔl/	fell /fɛl/	fallen /ˈfɔlən/
find /faɪnd/	found /faʊnd/	found /faʊnd/
fly /flaɪ/	flew /flu/	flown /floʊn/
forget /fərˈgɛt/	forgot /fərˈgɑt/	forgotten /fərˈgɑt(ə)n/
get /gɛt/	got /gɑt/	got /gɑt/, gotten /ˈgɑt(ə)n/
give /gɪv/	gave /geɪv/	given /ˈgɪv(ə)n/
go /goʊ/	went /wɛnt/	gone /gɔn/
have /hæv/	had /həd/	had /həd/
hear /hɪr/	heard /hɜrd/	heard /hɜrd/
know /noʊ/	knew /nu/	known /noʊn/
learn /lɜrn/	learnt / learned /lɜrnt/, /ˈlɜrnəd/	learnt / learned /lɜrnt/, /ˈlɜrnəd/
leave /liv/	left /lɛft/	left /lɛft/
lose /luz/	lost /lɔst/	lost /lɔst/
make /meɪk/	made /meɪd/	made /meɪd/
meet /mit/	met /mɛt/	met /mɛt/
pay /peɪ/	paid /peɪd/	paid /peɪd/
put /pʊt/	put /pʊt/	put /pʊt/
read /rid/	read /rɛd/	read /rɛd/
run /rʌn/	ran /ræn/	run /rʌn/
say /seɪ/	said /sɛd/	said /sɛd/
see /si/	saw /sɔ/	seen /sin/
sell /sɛl/	sold /soʊld/	sold /soʊld/
sing /sɪŋ/	sang /sæŋ/	sung /sʌŋ/
sit /sɪt/	sat /sæt/	sat /sæt/
speak /spik/	spoke /spoʊk/	spoken /ˈspoʊkən/
take /teɪk/	took /tʊk/	taken /ˈteɪkən/
teach /titʃ/	taught /tɔt/	taught /tɔt/
tell /tɛl/	told /toʊld/	told /toʊld/
think /θɪŋk/	thought /θɔt/	thought /θɔt/
wear /wɛr/	wore /wɔr/	worn /wɔrn/
win /wɪn/	won /wʌn/	won /wʌn/
write /raɪt/	wrote /roʊt/	written /ˈrɪt(ə)n/

WORKBOOK

CONTENTS

Unit 5 – Ambitions	**202**
Vocabulary 1 | Life Events	202
Grammar 1 | *will / won't*	203
Vocabulary 2 | Musical Instruments	205
Grammar 2 | First Conditional	206
Grammar Check	207
Listening	207
Extension	208
Vocabulary Plus | Other Life Events	209
Unit 6 – On Screen	**210**
Vocabulary 1 | Movies	210
Grammar 1 | Future Form: *will*; Future Form: *be going to*	211
Vocabulary 2 | Suffixes *-ion* and *-ment*	213
Grammar 2 | Review: Present Progressive for Future Arrangements	214
Grammar Check	215
Listening	215
Extension	216
Vocabulary Plus | The Movie Theater	217
Unit 7 – The World We Live in	**218**
Vocabulary 1 | Materials and Containers	218
Grammar 1 | Present Perfect (Affirmative and Negative)	219
Vocabulary 2 | Endangered Animals	221
Grammar 2 | Present Perfect (Questions and Short Answers)	222
Grammar Check	223
Listening	223
Extension	224
Vocabulary Plus | The Natural World	225
Unit 8 – Altruism	**226**
Vocabulary 1 | Fundraising Ideas	226
Grammar 1 | Present Perfect: *ever, never, yet, already, just*	227
Vocabulary 2 | *make* and *do*	229
Grammar 2 | Present Perfect: *for* and *since*	230
Grammar Check	231
Listening	231
Extension	232
Vocabulary Plus | Money	233

5 AMBITIONS

VOCABULARY 1

Life Events

1 Match the words with the verbs in the box to make phrases.

> be   buy   get (×2)
> go   have   learn
> leave (×2)   start   train   work

__leave__ school at 18

a _____ children
b _____ to drive
c _____ born
d _____ to be a vet
e _____ with children
f _____ a job
g _____ school at 6am
h _____ a house
i _____ married
j _____ to college
k _____ home

2 Label the pictures with the phrases in activity 1.

learn to drive   a _____
b _____   c _____
d _____   e _____
f _____   g _____
h _____   i _____
j _____   k _____

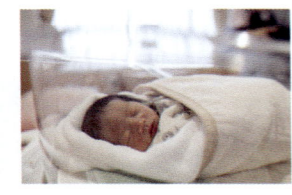

3 Complete the sentences using the words in activity 1.

a My sister wants to _____ on a beach in Hawaii. It's gonna be an awesome party!

b My best friend says she wants to _____ five _____! I'd like two: a boy and a girl.

c Rosie plans to _____ when she's older. She loves animals!

d My brother's nearly sixteen; he can _____ in dad's car.

e The oldest person in the world _____ over a hundred years ago.

f I want to _____ when I leave school. I'd like to study math!

202 two hundred two

UNIT 5

GRAMMAR 1

will / won't

1 Order the words to write sentences and add *will* or *'ll*.

as / brother / work / an / My / engineer
My brother will work as an engineer.

a me / lend / dad / money / and / for / a / present / Mom
_____

b a / You / new / need / USB hub
_____

c after / go / bed / the / I / news / to
_____

d college / We / before / travel
_____

e Matt / lot / have / children / a / of
_____

2 Write the sentences in activity 1 in the negative form.

My brother won't work as an engineer.

a _____
b _____
c _____
d _____
e _____

3 Look at the pictures and complete the predictions with *will* or *won't* and the verbs in parentheses.

Joanna ____will study____ science at college. (study)

a Amy _____ married to a short, blond man. (get)

b Pippa _____ how to drive a truck. (learn)

c Alfie _____ a famous athlete. (become)

d Mark _____ Japan. (visit)

e Michelle _____ a fast car. (buy)

4 Complete the dialogue with *'ll*, *will*, or *won't* and the verbs in the box.

| be   die   get   get married   give   go |
| have   not want   not work   train |

Iain Did you see *Family Secrets* last night?
Chloe Yes, it was exciting! I think Joey **a** _____ in the next episode. He's very sick.
Iain No, I don't agree! I think he **b** _____ better! The doctor **c** _____ him some amazing medicine. She **d** _____ to Brazil and buy it there.
Chloe Yes! And Brad **e** _____ to Patsy. They **f** _____ a big wedding.
Iain Yes, and Brad's mother **g** _____ really angry. She **h** _____ Brad and Patsy to be together.
Chloe And what about Clint, Joey's brother?
Iain Well, I think he **i** _____ as a lifeguard any more after the accident. He **j** _____ to be a nurse at the hospital.
Chloe Then Clint and the doctor will fall in love.
Iain Exactly!

5 Complete the sentences so they are true for you.

a When I'm 17, I _____.
b Next week, I _____.
c My favorite team _____.
d When I'm older, I won't _____.

two hundred three 203

6 Order the words to make questions.

   a she / Will / tomorrow / class / in / be ?
      Will she be in class tomorrow?

   b later / you / call / Will / me ?
      _____

   c know / I / the / answer / Will ?
      _____

   d be / difficult / Will / the / test ?
      _____

   e married / Will / next / they / get / year ?
      _____

   f homework / be / Will / today / there ?
      _____

7 Match the questions in activity 6 with the short answers.

   [d] Yes, it will.
   [ ] Yes, she will.
   [ ] No, there won't.
   [ ] No, you won't.
   [ ] Yes, they will.
   [ ] No, I won't.

8 Write questions with _will_.

   I / pass / the exam?
   Will I pass the exam?

   a he / get / the / job?
      _____

   b you / learn / to drive / a truck?
      _____

   c the new mouse / cost / a lot of money?
      _____

   d the vacation / be / boring?
      _____

   e we / buy / a house / by the sea?
      _____

9 Look at the pictures of what will happen in the future and write short answers for the questions in activity 8.

Yes, you will.   **a** _____

b _____   **c** _____

d _____   **e** _____

10 Write questions with _you_ for the answers using _will_ and the words in the box.

> How   What   Where   Who

   a _____
      We'll go to Costa Rica next summer.

   b _____
      Kelly will come with us.

   c _____
      We'll go there by plane.

   d _____
      I'll buy some shoes.

11 Answer the questions in activity 10 for you.

   a _____
   b _____
   c _____
   d _____

UNIT 5

VOCABULARY 2

Musical Instruments

1 Find eleven musical instruments in the wordsnake.

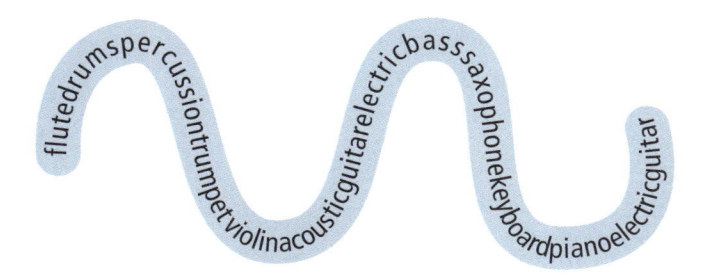

flute drums percussion trumpet violin acoustic guitar electric bass saxophone keyboard piano electric guitar

2 Look at the picture and label the instruments with the words in activity 1.

- a ___percussion___
- b _____
- c _____
- d _____
- e _____
- f _____
- g _____
- h _____
- i _____
- j _____
- k _____

3 Read the clues and write the words.

a You usually sit to play this instrument. It has four legs. It doesn't need electricity. _____

b You sit to play this instrument. You hit it with sticks or with your hands, and it's very loud! _____

c You usually hold this with your left hand and you rest it on your shoulder. _____

d You play this instrument with your mouth. Your hands go in front of you. It can be made of different materials. _____

e A lot of rock bands use this 4-string instrument. You need speakers to hear it. You play it with your fingers. _____

f This instrument can sound like a lot of different instruments. You play it with your hands. _____

4 Complete the sentences for you.

a In a pop band, my favorite instrument is the _____.

b In an orchestra, my favorite instrument is the _____.

c I don't like the _____.

d I have a friend who can play the _____.

GRAMMAR 2

First Conditional

1 Underline the correct options.

We **celebrate** / **'ll celebrate** if dad gets the job.

a If my sister **has** / **will have** children, I'll be an aunt!

b I **buy** / **'ll buy** a house near the beach if I earn a lot of money.

c If you **buy** / **'ll buy** a laptop, you won't need new speakers.

d If the rain **doesn't** / **won't** stop, we won't go camping.

e I won't go out tonight if there **'s** / **will be** something good on TV.

f If you **won't** / **don't** do your homework now, you'll have to do it later.

2 Complete the sentences with the first conditional form of the verbs in parentheses.

If you wear those clothes, you ___will feel___ cold. (feel)

a If you play that song again, he _____ happy. (not be)

b I _____ you if you go to the hospital. (visit)

c If you don't hurry, you _____ time for lunch. (not have)

d If I _____ his T-shirt, I'll buy it. (see)

e She won't go to college if she _____. (not study)

3 Write sentences with the first conditional form.

a go to the city / visit the museum
_____

b get a job / earn extra money
_____

c fail her exams / not go to college
_____

d go to college / study art
_____

e have enough money / see a movie
_____

f become a taxi driver / drive a pink taxi
_____

4 Match the beginnings to the endings.

a If you pass your exams,
b If I go out in the rain,
c Will it be warmer
d If we change school,
e Will you tell them

☐ will we have a uniform?
☐ if we build a fire?
☐ if you see them?
☐a will your parents be happy?
☐ will I catch a cold?

5 Complete the questions with the first conditional form of the verbs in parentheses.

If you __come__ (come) home early, __will__ you __make__ (make) lunch?

a _____ you _____ (send) me a postcard if you _____ (have) time?

b If I _____ (tell) you a secret, _____ you _____ (tell) everybody?

c _____ grandma _____ (learn) to drive if dad _____ (help) her?

d If they _____ (visit) us, _____ they _____ (bring) the dog?

6 Complete the dialogue with the first conditional form of the verbs in the box. Complete the short answers.

> do   get   go   not be
> not have   not leave   want

Ben a _____ you _____ to college if you b _____ school at 18?

Lola Yes, c _____. I want to study to be a vet. What d _____ you _____ if you can?

Ben I'll get a job. If you e _____ enough money as a student, f _____ you _____ a weekend job?

Lola No, g _____. If I h _____ to be a vet, there i _____ time for a job!

206 two hundred six

UNIT 5

GRAMMAR CHECK

1 Read the dialogue and circle the correct answers.

Anna I think I **a** _____ to that concert tonight. **b** _____ fun. Do you want to come?

Maddy If we **c** _____ a lot of homework, we won't have time.

Anna I'll do my homework after school. I don't have a lot. It **d** _____ four hours!

Maddy Well, if my dad **e** _____ it's alright, I'll come. Who's playing?

Anna Some friends of Ben's. He says if we go, we **f** _____ it.

Maddy OK. I **g** _____ my dad. If I do my homework early, it **h** _____ be a problem.

Anna Awesome! Oh, one more thing. If **i** _____ expensive, **j** _____ me some money?

	1	2	3
a	go	going	('ll go)
b	It is	It'll be	It be
c	has	have	will have
d	don't take	to take	won't take
e	will say	says	say
f	'll enjoy	enjoys	enjoy
g	ask	'll ask	am asking
h	won't	isn't	don't
i	it's	is	its
j	will you lend	you will lend	do you lend

2 Listen and check your answers.

13))

LISTENING

1 Listen to the dialogue and answer the questions.

14))

a What do the people on the show do?
_____

b Who does Aisha like?
_____

c Who does Callum like?
_____

2 Listen again and underline the correct words.

14))

a Last year, the winner of the show was a **violin / saxophone** player.

b Callum heard about the show **at school / on the internet**.

c Aisha's favorite singer wears the **most expensive / most creative** clothes.

d Aisha's favorite singer is **older / younger** than Callum's favorite singer.

e Callum's favorite singer plays the **guitar / piano**.

f If Callum's favorite wins, she'll buy **a house / a restaurant**.

g Aisha's favorite singer wants to win to **help her family / be famous**.

two hundred seven 207

EXTENSION

Underline the correct options to complete the text.

Jane Austen's house in Chawton, England. Now it is a museum.

If you **a like / will like** classic novels, you **b enjoy / 'll enjoy** Jane Austen. Austen is one of the most famous writers in English literature, and she **c was / were** born in 1775. She only **d was / went** to school for one year, and she didn't **e go / went** to university, but her father and brothers were her teachers at home and she read **f a lot of / much** books. Her ambition was to work as a writer. She practiced a lot, and, when she was 35 years old, she **g write / wrote** her first novel, *Sense and Sensibility*. This is one of her **h best / most good** novels. When Jane was writing, women of her social class spent their time visiting friends and family or at dances. Typically, the **i more important / most important** ambition for men and women was to get married. Jane wrote about these people, but she was ironic and laughed at society. Her stories and characters **j is / are** still popular today and probably will **k be / to be** for a long time. You **l should / will** read one of her novels.

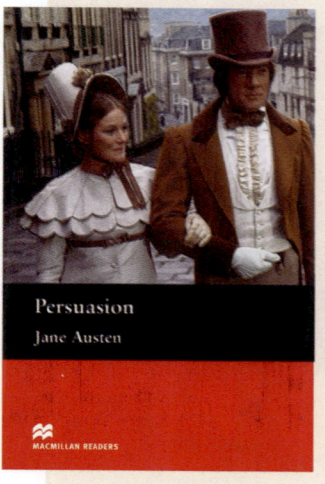

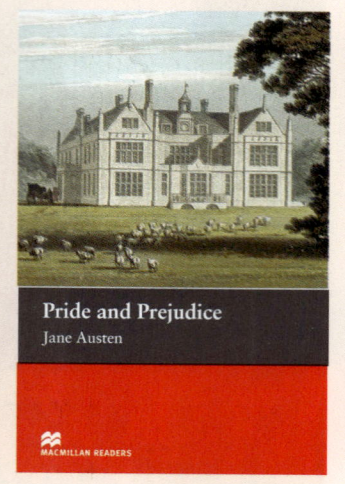

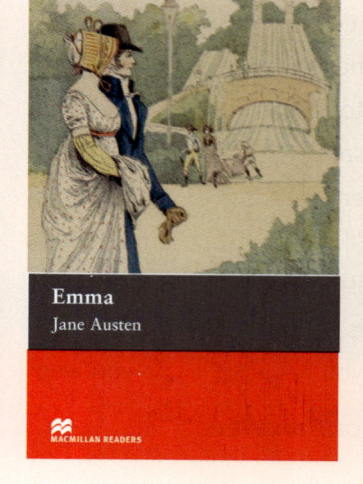

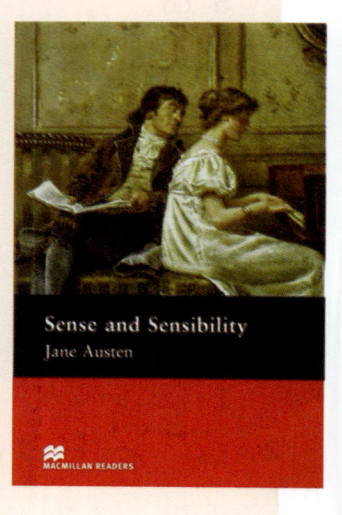

Jane Austen best known novels.

UNIT 5

VOCABULARY PLUS

Other Life Events

1 _____
2 _____
3 _____
4 _____
5 _____
6 _____
7 _____

1 Listen to the words and repeat.

2 Translate the following words into your language.

a anniversary: _____
b birth: _____
c death: _____
d divorce: _____
e engagement: _____
f funeral: _____
g retirement: _____
h wedding: _____

3 Label the pictures with the words in activity 2. Which life event is not in the pictures?
_____

4 Complete these sentences with a word from activity 2.

Do you know what sort of flowers the bride is having at her __wedding__?

a My parents got married in May 2000. It's their wedding _____ tomorrow.

b My uncle's going to stop working next week. He's having a _____ party.

c Our family is having a party next week to celebrate my older brother's _____.

d When my aunt died, I went to her _____.

e Jack and Kerry got married in 1996. Three years later, they got a _____.

f Tahani and Kurt invited their closest friends to celebrate the _____ of their first child.

6 ON SCREEN

VOCABULARY 1

Movies

1 Complete the words with the vowels.

d _i_ r _e_ ct _o_ r

a st __ nt d __ __ bl __

b m __ v __ __ st __ r

c scr __ __ n

d sp __ c __ __ l __ ff __ cts

2 Find five movie words in the wordsnake and match them with the definitions.

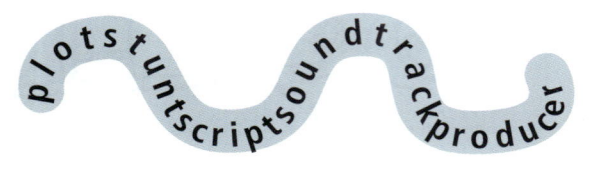

plotstuntscriptsoundtrackproducer

a the words of a movie
_____

b a dangerous action in a movie
_____

c the music of a movie
_____

d the story of a movie
_____

e the person who organizes the money for a movie
_____

3 Complete the phrases with the verbs in the box.

| film   release   star   win |

a _____ in a movie
b _____ an award
c _____ a movie
d _____ a scene

4 What are they talking about? Match the words in the box with the sentences.

| movie star   ~~plot~~   soundtrack   special effects
streaming platform   stunt double |

It's a really good story, with a twist at the end.
_____plot_____

a I loved the song when they were standing in the front of the ship. It was very romantic.
_____

b I love it because I can watch movies in the comfort of my home.
_____

c It's amazing when the gorilla picks her up and carries her up that tall building. How did they do that?
_____

d She's amazingly rich and famous. She got $15 million dollars for her part in that movie.
_____

e The director made him jump out of the helicopter and ski down the mountain instead of the star.
_____

5 Complete the sentences with the words in the box.

| award   ~~director~~   release   scene   star |

Chloé Zhao is a well-known ___director___. *Eternals* was directed by her.

a They filmed the desert _____ in Morocco.

b An Oscar is another word for an Academy _____.

c Tom Holland and Zendaya _____ in *Spider-Man: No Way Home*.

d When are they going to _____ the new Marvel movie?

UNIT 6

🔑 GRAMMAR 1

Future Form: *will*

1 Order the words to make sentences.

change / probably / movie / life / This / will / your
<u>This movie will probably change your life.</u>

a and terrifying / brilliant / find / it / will / You / definitely
_____
_____

b a / be / bored / for / minute / won't / definitely / You
_____
_____

c probably / come out / streaming / movie / for / months / on / six / The / won't
_____
_____

d after / become / teen actor / definitely / famous / movie / The / this / will
_____
_____

e castle / ever / forget / in / Nobody / the scene / the / will
_____
_____

2 Complete the sentences with *will* and the verbs in the box.

be   love   make (2×)
pay   release   watch

a In the coming years, movies _____ much more use of technology to create special effects.

b You _____ this movie. It's amazing.

c It's a great movie, but it _____ you cry.

d People _____ more for movie tickets in the future.

e In the future, there _____ new trends making 3D movies popular again.

f One day, the movie industry _____ movies only on streaming platforms.

g In the future, everybody _____ 3D movies without glasses.

3 Match the sentence beginnings with the endings. Write sentences using *won't* and the verbs in parentheses.

a [5] We (be) late for the movie, I …
b [ ] You (enjoy) that movie because you …
c [ ] He's an excellent stunt double, so …
d [ ] We (understand) the movie because it's …
e [ ] There'll be advertisements first, so …
f [ ] Don't worry – the bad guys (win) because …

1 all in Japanese.
2 he (hurt) himself.
3 they never do!
4 don't like romantic movies.
5 promise you.
6 the movie (start) at eight.

a <u>We won't be late for the movie, I promise you.</u>
b _____
c _____
d _____
e _____
f _____

4 Write questions with *will*. Then answer them with your opinions using *will* or *won't*.

In the year 2200 …

the world / be much hotter?
Will the world be much hotter?
Yes, it will be much hotter. / No, it won't be much hotter.

a people / take vacations on Mars?
_____
_____

b there / be more deserts in Europe?
_____
_____

c the sea / cover half of the continent?
_____
_____

d we / travel everywhere by bicycle?
_____
_____

Future Form: *be going to*

5 Complete the sentences with the correct form of *be going to* and the verbs in parentheses.

"Have you seen that new Argentinian movie yet?"

"No, but I ___'m going to see___ (see) it soon. It sounds excellent."

a I _____ (study) to be a cameraman when I leave school.

b Why are you holding that camera? _____ (you / make) a movie of us?

c Angie and Colin want to go to the USA next summer. They _____ (buy) a car when they get there, and they _____ (travel) from the East Coast to the West.

d I don't like this actor, so I _____ (not see) her new movie.

e "I'm going to a party tonight." "What _____ (you / wear)?"

f This movie is awful! It _____ (not win) any awards.

6 You have decided to change things in your life next year. What things are you going to change? Write four sentences.

I'm going to get up early every day. I'm not going to eat too much candy.
_____

a _____
_____
_____

b _____
_____
_____

c _____
_____
_____

d _____
_____
_____

UNIT 6

VOCABULARY 2

Suffixes -ion and -ment

1 Make nouns ending in -ion or -ment from these verbs.

verbs	nouns
advertise	advertisement
a decorate	_____
b enjoy	_____
c equip	_____
d possess	_____
e excite	_____
f suggest	_____

2 Make verbs from these nouns.

nouns	verbs
education	educate
a argument	_____
b competition	_____
c information	_____
d development	_____
e connection	_____
f prediction	_____

3 Label the pictures with two nouns from activity 1 and two verbs from activity 2.

a  _____   b _____

c  _____   d _____

4 Match the nouns in the box with the sentences.

> advertisement   ~~argument~~   development
> education   information   prediction
> suggestion

"The Government should ban cars in the center of Montreal." "No. That's a ridiculous idea. Some people live in the center and they need a car if they have to bring heavy shopping home."
___argument___

a Buy Meow! It's a new kind of cat food, and cats LOVE it! _____

b By the year 2080, there will be a vacation hotel on Mars. _____

c Why don't we make some sandwiches and go for a picnic by the river? _____

d When I leave school, I'd like to go to college. I want to get a degree in law. _____

e Ten years ago, there wasn't any water in that African village. Now, they have it and the people are much healthier. _____

f Trains from Platform 2 are for London only. _____

5 Complete the sentences with the nouns in the box.

> competition   connection   decoration
> enjoyment   ~~equipment~~   excitement
> possession

Can I borrow your camping __equipment__ next week, please? I have a sleeping bag, but I don't have anything else.

a I couldn't hear him when he called because the _____ was very bad.

b I love this silver necklace. It is my favorite _____.

c This room needs some _____ for the party – maybe flowers, candles, and balloons.

d Your photo of the sunset is amazing. You should send it to the photo _____ in this magazine.

e My aunt gets a lot of _____ from her garden. She's always happy when she is working in it.

f There was a lot of _____ at school today because a movie crew was filming in some of the classes.

two hundred thirteen 213

GRAMMAR 2

Review: Present Progressive for Future Arrangements

1 Look at Andy's diary and complete the questions and answers using the present progressive.

Day	Saturday	Sunday
morning	Meet Rob at 11 to practice our new song.	Go for a run in the park with Adam.
afternoon	Play tennis with Adam from 2 to 4.	Finish science project.
evening	Take Kate to the movies – pick her up at 6.	Meet Kate at Moonshine at 7 for a meal.

Who __is Andy meeting__ on Saturday morning?
He's __meeting__ Rob.

a What time _____ tennis with Adam?
They _____ from two to four.

b Who _____ to the movies on Saturday evening?
He _____ Kate.

c What _____ and Adam _____ on Sunday morning?
They _____ for a run in the park.

d What _____ on Sunday afternoon?
He _____ his science project.

e Where _____ Andy and Kate _____ at seven on Sunday?
They _____ at Moonshine.

2 Complete the sentences with the present progressive form of the verbs in parentheses.

Today at 9pm Melissa __is throwing__ a party to celebrate the movie release. (throw)

a I _____ lunch with my friends near the movie theater today. (have)

b _____ Peter _____ to the movies at 2pm or at 3pm on Saturday? (go)

c The cast _____ the main scene tonight. (rehearse)

d My sister _____ all of the series next month. (watch)

e The trailers _____ in a few moments. Hurry up! (start)

f The director _____ a new stunt double in fifteen days. (interview)

3 What definite plans do you have for this weekend? Write five sentences about your plans using the present progressive.

On Saturday I'm meeting my friends for a meal at the Oasis.

a _____
b _____
c _____
d _____
e _____

UNIT 6

GRAMMAR CHECK

1 Read the text and circle the correct answers.

When I leave school, **a** _____ probably go to college. I **b** _____ to study modern languages, I think. Then if I **c** _____ a good degree, **d** _____ to get a job with a movie or TV company for a few years. After that, when I've saved some money, I **e** _____ apply to a film school. If **f** _____ possible, **g** _____ go to film school in Los Angeles. I love the USA. **h** _____ the whole of next month in California with my aunt Melanie. Oliver, one of my friends, **i** _____ with me. I can't wait. We **j** _____ a lot of fun there!

	1	2	3
a	I	I'm	(I'll)
b	'm going	going	go
c	will get	get	got
d	I try	I tried	I'll try
e	go to	'm going to	'll go
f	it was	it will be	it's
g	I'll	I	I'm going
h	I'll spend	I spend	I'm spending
i	comes	is coming	will come
j	're going to have	're having	'll having

2 Listen and check your answers.
16))

LISTENING

1 Listen and circle T for *true* or F for *false*.
17))

a Auguste and Louis Lumière were brothers. **T / F**
b At their first public movie show, the audience didn't have to pay. **T / F**
c The cinematographe was a camera and a projector. **T / F**
d People say *Baby's Breakfast* was the world's first comedy movie. **T / F**
e *The Arrival of a Train at a Station* was a very realistic movie. **T / F**
f The Lumières only filmed real-life situations. **T / F**
g The Lumières never left France. **T / F**
h Louis Lumière said the cinema was never going to become popular. **T / F**

Auguste Marie Louis Nicolas Lumière   Louis Jean Lumière

2 Listen again and answer the questions.
17))

a In what year was the first public movie shown?
_____
b How long was it?
_____
c How much did the cinematographe weigh?
_____
d How many movies were there in the show?
_____
e What did the first movie show?
_____
f What was the first comedy movie called?
_____
g Which cities did they tour with their movies?
_____
h How many Lumière movies were there by 1900?
_____

two hundred fifteen 215

EXTENSION

Circle the correct options to complete the text.

a I've spent / I was spending the last two years watching old movies whenever I get the chance. I love
b watch / watching them. **c** I've done / I did this **d** since / from I was 13, when I was in bed for a week with a broken leg. During the winter, I **e** often stay / am often staying in all day on Sundays to watch old classics. Last Sunday, I **f** watched / have watched half of *Gone with the Wind*. It was **g** too / very long to watch it all, so
h I'm going / I will to watch the rest of it next Sunday. My friend Renata **i** is coming / will come to stay next weekend so she'll probably **j** watching / watch it with me. If we **k** have / will have time,
l we watch / we'll watch *Casablanca* afterwards. **m** I've already seen / I already saw it twice, but I think it's the **n** best / better movie of all time. When I finish school and university, I'm going to get a job as a movie reviewer.
o I'll spend / I'm spending every day at the movie theater and **p** I'll get / I'm getting paid for it. How
q much / more fun will that be? Not **r** lot / many people in the world get paid to watch movies, do they?

UNIT 6

VOCABULARY PLUS

The Movie Theater

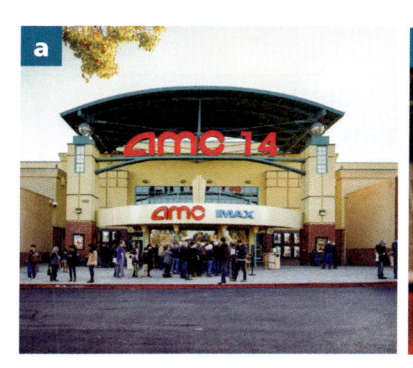

a _____   b _____   c _____

d _____   g _____   i _____   j _____
e _____   h _____
f _____

1 Label the pictures with the words in the box. Then listen and repeat.

autograph	popcorn
box office	seat
Hollywood blockbuster	soft drink
movie premiere	ticket
multiplex movie theater	trailer

2 Complete the definitions with the correct options.

A _Hollywood blockbuster_ is an American movie that is extremely popular.

a A _____ is a movie theater that has a lot of different screens.

b A _____ is an extract from a movie that will be released soon.

c The _____ is the place where you buy your movie ticket.

d A _____ is the first time a movie is shown in a country.

e _____ is a popular snack that people eat at the movies.

f An _____ is a signature that a celebrity write in objects, when fans ask them.

3 Circle the correct options.

I love watching the **box offices** / **trailers** before the main movie starts.

a "Would you like a **soft drink** / **seat**?" "Yes, please. A Coke."

b "Two **tickets** / **trailers** for *Minions: The Rise of Gru*, please." "That's 30 dollars, please."

c We don't like sitting in the **movie premieres** / **seats** directly below the screen.

d The movie premiere was fantastic. I'm sure it'll be a **soft drink** / **Hollywood blockbuster**.

e I asked a movie star for his **popcorn** / **autograph** and he signed my T-shirt!

two hundred seventeen 217

7

THE WORLD WE LIVE IN

ABC VOCABULARY 1

Materials and Containers

1 Find fourteen materials and containers in the word search.

L	P	C	A	R	T	O	N	B	I	A
M	P	A	P	O	R	Y	W	O	O	L
S	L	R	P	L	N	U	H	X	E	U
J	A	D	L	E	S	A	S	E	E	M
A	S	B	T	O	R	B	E	T	W	I
R	T	O	W	M	N	O	L	E	H	N
F	I	A	R	S	E	T	C	M	O	U
H	C	R	C	O	T	T	O	N	P	M
I	D	D	A	O	G	L	A	S	S	Z
B	A	G	N	R	M	E	N	L	C	S

2 Match the columns to make compound nouns. Then complete the sentences.

- a cardboard   ☐ T-shirt
- b wool   a box
- c plastic   ☐ can
- d cotton   ☐ bag
- e metal   ☐ sweater

1 My cat likes sleeping in a ___cardboard box___.
2 It's cold today, so he's wearing a _____.
3 If you go to the market, you'll need a _____.
4 For PE, I always wear a cool _____.
5 Soft drinks are often in _____.

3 Complete the text with the words in the box.

| aluminum | bottles | cartons |
| cotton | glass | jars | paper |

Hi! I'm Mateo. In my family, we always try to recycle. It's good for the planet! We wash plastic **a** _____ and use them again for water, and we use **b** _____ in the kitchen for rice, beans, and sugar. We put all our **c** _____ cans in the recycling bins outside the supermarket. Milk and juice **d** _____ can't be recycled in my town, so we buy these things in **e** _____ bottles. My mother sometimes gives old clothes to other people, and she sometimes cuts up **f** _____ clothes and uses them in the kitchen. We ask for **g** _____ bags in the supermarket, not plastic. Or even better, we take our own bags. How does your family recycle?

4 Complete the sentences for you. Use words from activity 1.

- a In my family we recycle _____.
- b We don't really need to use _____.
- c It'll be difficult to stop using _____.
- d When I was younger, I sometimes played with _____.

UNIT 7

🔑 GRAMMAR 1

Present Perfect (Affirmative and Negative)

1 Write the past participles. Which three verbs are regular?

verb	past participle
open	_opened_
a be	_____
b build	_____
c buy	_____
d fall	_____
e have	_____
f take	_____
g stop	_____
h try	_____

Opened, _____, and _____ are regular.

2 Underline the correct words.

I **has** / **have** stopped using plastic bags.

a We **has** / **have** reduced our garbage at home.

b I **has** / **have** used this plastic bag about ten times.

c My brother **has** / **have** recycled his old school T-shirt.

d My parents **has** / **have** watched three hours of Netflix today.

e The dog **has** / **have** eaten my homework!

3 Complete the sentences with the present perfect affirmative form of the verbs in parentheses.

We _'ve had_ our lunch. (have)

a I _____ to find a recycling bin for cans. (try)

b She _____ the ice cream in the sun. (leave)

c They _____ a store that sells organic cotton clothes. (open)

d He _____ very famous. (become)

e We _____ old CDs in the garden. (use)

f You _____ all the cake! (eat)

4 Look at the pictures and write sentences about them with the present perfect form of the verbs in the box.

| break | build | buy |
| cut | eat | fall |

a _____

b _____

c _____

d _____

e _____

f _____

5 Complete the sentences for you.

a The best place I've visited was _____.

b I've met _____.

c I've never _____.

d My friend has _____ today.

two hundred nineteen 219

6 Complete the sentences with *haven't* or *hasn't*.

The film ____hasn't____ started. Quick, sit down.

a I _____ heard their new song.
b She _____ cleaned her teeth!
c We _____ seen him today.
d My brother _____ passed his math test.
e They _____ reduced their screen time.
f My cat _____ eaten its dinner.

7 Rewrite the sentences using the information in parentheses.

It's been hot in the last few days. (cold)
It hasn't been hot in the last few days.
It's been cold.

a My teacher has tried sushi. (shark)
_____
_____

b She's taken your camera. (cell phone)
_____
_____

c I've seen Tom Holland. (Benedict Cumberbatch)
_____
_____

d We've visited New York. (London)
_____
_____

e They've traveled by boat. (by plane)
_____
_____

f He's adopted an elephant. (dolphin)
_____
_____

8 Complete the dialogue with the present perfect form of the verbs in parentheses.

Jordan I **a** _____ (not see) Tom in the last few days. He **b** _____ (not come) to guitar class at all this week.

Elliot We **c** _____ (have) exams at school so he **d** _____ (be) very busy.

Jordan Oh, OK. We had exams too, but we **e** _____ (finish) them all now. I **f** _____ (pass) all my subjects except one.

Elliot Which one?

Jordan Math.

Elliot Tom **g** _____ (not pass) math either. He knows it because he couldn't answer a lot of questions. And I don't know if I **h** _____ (pass) it. I **i** _____ (study) a lot, so I think it'll be OK.

Jordan Good luck!

9 Complete the sentences for you.

a I've never been to _____.
b My best friend hasn't _____ this week.
c My parents haven't _____ before.
d I haven't _____ today.

UNIT 7

VOCABULARY 2

Endangered Animals

1 Order the letters and write the words.

    k a n e s   ____snake____
  a h n o r e o s i c r _____
  b p l e d o r a   _____
  c d a n a p   _____
  d l o p r a r a b e   _____
  e t r e g i   _____
  f p l o d i h n   _____
  g p a e l e t h n   _____
  h r u t t l e   _____
  i g o r n a a t u n   _____

2 Look at the pictures and label the animals with the words from activity 1.

a _____ b _____

c _____ d _____

e _____ f _____

g _____ h _____

i _____ j _____

3 Write the animals from activity 1 in the correct group.

animals that live on land
snake,

animals that live in water

animals that live on land and in water

4 Read the clues and write the words.

  a I live in China. I am in danger of extinction. I eat bamboo. I am black and white. What am I? _____

  b I live in water and on land. I lay eggs. I have a shell. What am I? _____

  c I'm a mammal. I'm a good hunter. I'm from the same family as a cat. I have stripes. What am I? _____

  d I have four legs, but I can't jump. I have big ears and my Indian cousins have smaller ears. I have a shower with my nose. What am I? _____

  e I live in the forest. My hands are similar to human hands. I'm very intelligent and I live in Southeast Asia. What am I? _____

  f I live in the Arctic but not in the Antarctic. I eat meat and fish. I'm very big. What am I? _____

5 Complete the sentences for you.

  a My favorite endangered animal is the _____.

  b I don't like the _____.

  c I like the _____ better than the _____.

  d In a safari park, I visit the _____ first.

two hundred twenty-one **221**

GRAMMAR 2

Present Perfect (Questions and Short Answers)

1 Complete the questions with *have* or *has*. Then match the questions with the short answers.

a _____Has_____ Ms. Zimmer arrived?
b _____ I seen an orangutan?
c _____ we eaten all the cookies?
d _____ you put recycling bins in your kitchen?
e _____ he reused those jars?
f _____ they drunk my juice?

☐ Yes, they have.
[a] Yes, she has.
☐ No, we haven't.
☐ No, he hasn't.
☐ Yes, I have.
☐ No, you haven't.

2 Order the words to make questions. Then complete the short answers.

my / seen / you / Have / notebook?
Have you seen my notebook?
No, ____I haven't____.

a homework / rewritten / Have / you / your ?
_____
Yes, _____.

b cans and cartons / he / Has / his / recycled ?
_____
Yes, _____.

c he / told / Has / my sister ?
_____
No, _____.

d some / earned / I / extra allowance / Have ?
_____
No, _____.

e Have / out / they / taken / the garbage ?
_____
Yes, _____.

f Have / the cake / eaten / you ?
_____
Yes, _____.

3 Complete the questions with the present perfect form of the verbs in parentheses. Then complete the short answers.

Louis   a _____ (you / finish) your homework, Kyle?
Kyle   No, b _____.
Louis   But I want to play basketball with you.
        c _____ (you / start) it yet?
Kyle   Yes, I d _____. But I'm looking for my pencil case.
        e _____ (you / see) it?
Louis   Yes, I f _____. It's in the kitchen. I'll get it for you.
Kyle   Thanks.
Louis   g _____ (your teacher / give) you a lot of homework?
Kyle   Yes, he h _____.
Louis   Ooh. It looks difficult.
        i _____ (you / do) number four yet?
Kyle   No, I j _____.
        k _____ (you / finish) asking questions?
Louis   Why?
Kyle   Because I'm trying to do my homework!
Louis   Erp … sorry, hahaha!

4 Complete the questions using the phrases in the box or your own ideas. Write answers for you.

| eat shark | ride a camel |
| see a famous person | travel to another country |

a Have you ever _____?
b Have your parents ever _____?
c Has your friend ever _____?
d Has your teacher ever _____?

UNIT 7

GRAMMAR CHECK

1 Read the dialogue and circle the correct answers.

Josh How have **a** ___ your habits? Have you **b** ___ recycling?
Ben Yes, **c** ___. We've **d** ___ plastic boxes for meat and fish, so we **e** ___ plastic bags recently.
Josh Has your town **f** ___ recycling bins on your street?
Ben Yes, they have. And they've given us a new bin for food waste this week.
Josh Have you used the new bin?
Ben No, **g** ___, but we want to.
Josh What else **h** ___?
Ben To reduce energy use? We've **i** ___ our lights.
Josh That's great. Have you written about your changes in your blog?
Ben No, I haven't, but my sister **j** ___. I don't have a computer – they use electricity!

	1	2	3
a	you change	(you changed)	changed you
b	start	starting	started
c	we have	we have started	we started
d	buy	buying	bought
e	haven't needed	not need	not needed
f	put	to put	putting
g	you haven't	we haven't	we didn't
h	you've done	did you	have you done
i	changing	changed	change
j	did	was	has

2 Listen and check your answers.
19))

LISTENING

1 Listen to a radio show and underline the animals the speakers mention.
20))

> chimpanzees   crocodiles   lions   monkeys
> rhinoceroses   snakes   tigers   turtles

2 Listen again and write T for *true* or F for *false*.
20))
- **a** ☐ London Zoo opened in 1820.
- **b** ☐ London Zoo had the first children's zoo.
- **c** ☐ London Zoo has more than 750 different kinds of animals.
- **d** ☐ There aren't any elephants or rhinoceroses.
- **e** ☐ The monkey house is big.
- **f** ☐ Chris hasn't seen a real crocodile.
- **g** ☐ The only quagga in the world is in London Zoo.

EXTENSION

Underline the correct options to complete the text.

There **a is / are** a lot of different art forms, but there's one that combines sculpture and recycling: scrap-metal sculpture. It's a type of art that **b is becoming / becomes** more popular as people think more about recycling. **c You've / Have you** seen the movie *Wall-E*? **d Much / A lot of** scrap-metal sculptures look like that robot. In fact, making these sculptures is great fun and if you **e like / 'll like** science fiction, you **f love / 'll love** this art! You can invent aliens and robots, and you can make **g bigger / more big** sculptures **h than / that** with other materials.

You probably **i didn't / haven't** visited the biggest scrap-metal sculpture in the world, because it's in rural Wisconsin, in the north of the USA. However, the most famous scrap-metal sculpture in the world is probably Pablo Picasso's work. He **j did use / used** a recycled bicycle to make an animal. American artist John Chamberlain made the most colorful sculptures because he used to paint **k they / them**, and he is one of the most famous scrap-metal artists ever. Why not try scrap-metal sculpture? You'll have a lot of fun, you'll use your imagination, and you'll help the environment.

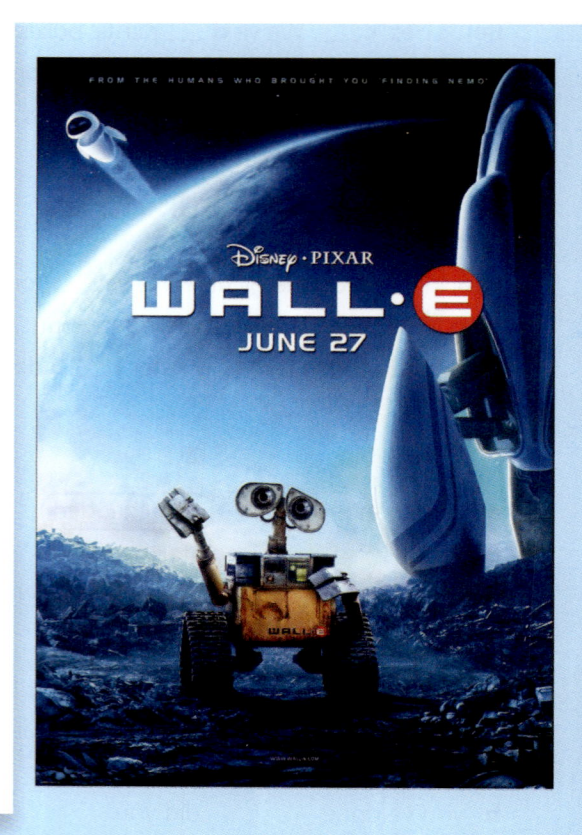

UNIT 7

ABC VOCABULARY PLUS

The Natural World

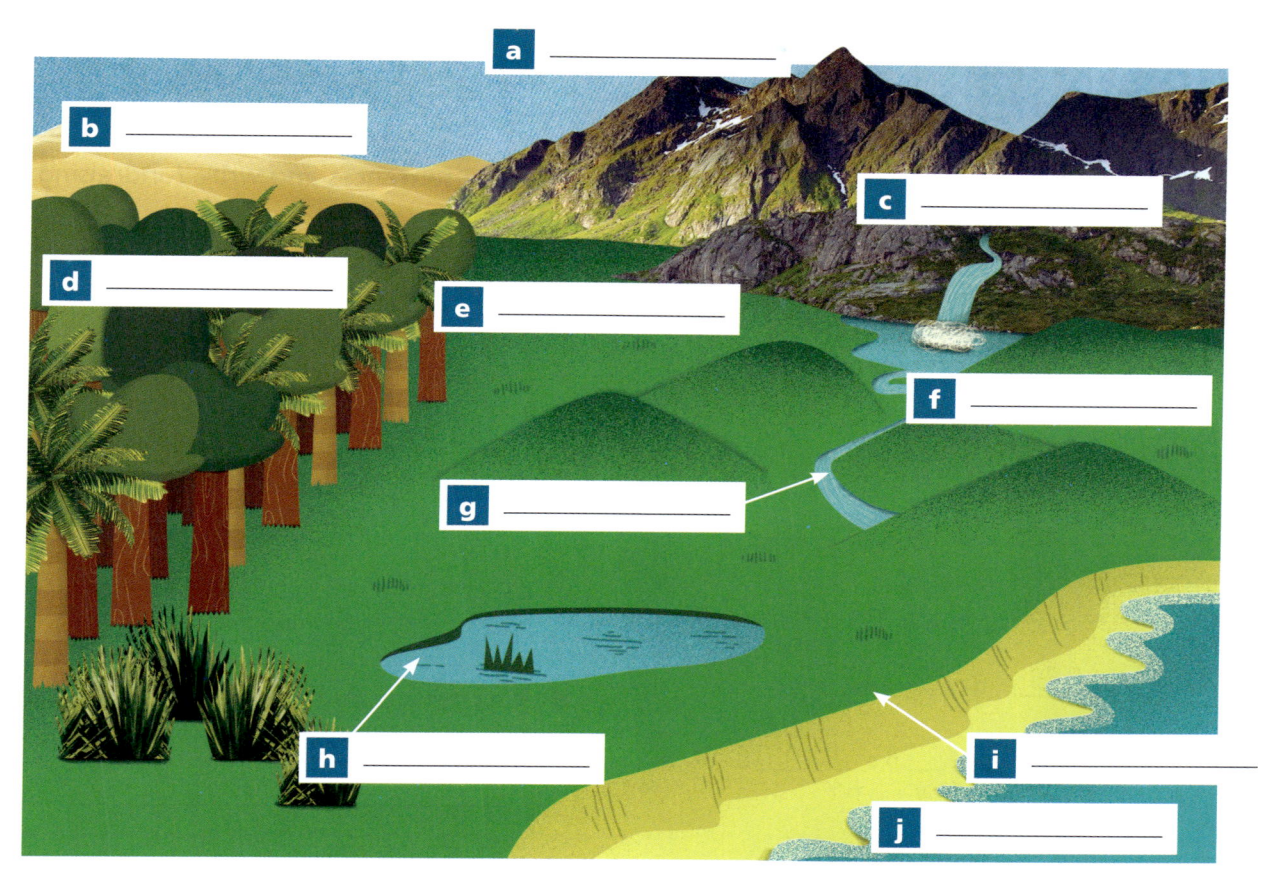

a _____
b _____
c _____
d _____
e _____
f _____
g _____
h _____
i _____
j _____

1 Check the meaning of the words in the box. Then listen and repeat.

| cliff   coast   desert   hill   mountain range |
| pond   rain forest   stream   valley   waterfall |

2 Label the picture with words from activity 1.

3 Find seven words in the word search.

K	S	T	R	E	A	M	C	K	V
W	A	T	E	R	F	A	L	L	A
M	K	G	R	D	W	H	I	A	L
D	E	S	E	R	T	K	F	L	L
C	O	A	S	T	A	V	F	F	E
P	O	N	D	D	M	M	Y	S	Y

4 Underline the correct word to complete the sentences.

We went to see the ____waterfalls____ of Iguazu.

<u>waterfalls</u>   streams   deserts

a The temperature in the Sahara _____ is often 58°C.
   1 stream   **2** desert   **3** valley

b The _____ is 2 meters deep.
   1 pond   **2** hill   **3** coast

c The Alps are the highest _____ in Europe.
   1 hill   **2** cliff   **3** mountain range

d People shouldn't chop down trees in the _____.
   1 rain forest   **2** stream   **3** desert

e We live on the _____. I can see the beach from my bedroom window.
   1 hill   **2** coast   **3** valley

two hundred twenty-five 225

8

ALTRUISM

ABC VOCABULARY 1

Fundraising Ideas

1 Complete the fundraising ideas with vowels.

a cr __ __ t __   __ n   __ n l __ n __
  cr __ w d f __ n d __ n g   p __ g __

b d __ n __ t __   f __ __ d

c d __ n __ t __   t __ y s

d h __ v __   __   c __ r   w __ s h   d __ y

e h __ v __   __   d __ g   w __ s h   d __ y

f h __ v __   __   s p __ n s __ r __ d   s p __ r t __ n g   __ v __ n t

g __ r g __ n __ z __   __   b __ n __ f __ t   c __ n c __ r t

h __ r g __ n __ z __   __ n   c __ m m __ n __ t y   y __ r d   s __ l __

2 Match fundraising ideas from activity 1 with the pictures.

a _____   b _____

c _____   d _____

3 Read the sentences and write fundraising ideas.

Do you have any old toys, clothes, or books? Could you sell them if you don't use them anymore?
organize a community yard sale

a The musicians are here. The audience is arriving. We're starting in five minutes.
_____

b It will take about half an hour. It will be lovely and clean when I finish.
_____

c It's for hungry children. Put it in the box, please. Thank you very much.
_____

d She's trying to do 1 kilometer. I'm paying her 1 dollar for every 100 meters. So, if she swims 1 kilometer, I have to give her 10 dollars.
_____

e They can wash your lovely Spot for 5 dollars. Could we take care of this little guy?
_____

f My friends and I are preparing the website online. We want to raise a lot of money for charity.
_____

g We're putting all of our toys together to give them to the children for the charity program.
_____

UNIT 8

🔑 GRAMMAR 1

Present Perfect: *ever, never, yet, already, just*

1 Rewrite the sentences with the words in parentheses.

I've lost my coin purse. (just)
I've just lost my coin purse.

a She has written to me. (never)
_____

b You've made a mistake. (just)
_____

c Has she been fired? (ever)
_____

d It's started to rain. (already)
_____

e She has not found it. (yet)
_____

f Have you told a lie? (ever)
_____

g We have had lunch. (already)
_____

h Have you eaten the chocolate? (yet)
_____

i They have visited the Great Wall of China. (never)
_____

2 Complete the sentences with the present perfect form of the verbs and the words in parentheses.

Dianne _____has just run_____ (run / just) 20 kilometers to raise money for charity.

a Dave _____ (write / already) 30 emails today.

b I _____ all the toys I have. (not donate)

c I _____ (see / just) a movie showing the terrible conditions in the refugee camps.

d They_____ (do / never) work for charities.

e You_____ (make / already) lots of money with your community yard sale.

3 Complete the answers to the questions with the present perfect form of the verbs in parentheses. Use *never* or *yet*.

Did he enjoy the sponsored walk?
I don't know. He __hasn't told__ (tell) me __yet__.

a What's the benefit concert like?
I don't know. _____ (watch) it _____.

b What did she think of the movie?
She _____ (see) it.

c Why are they so hungry?
They _____ (eat) anything _____.

d Are your new shoes comfortable?
I _____ (wear) them _____.

e When are we having the community yard sale?
I'm not sure because I_____ (speak) to Ellie about it.

4 Match the statements with the questions. Then complete the questions with the present perfect form of the verbs in parentheses. Use *yet* or *ever*.

a I want to do some charity work [2]
b It's Ryan's birthday tomorrow. [ ]
c Katy can't see the board. [ ]
d Let's go to the park. [ ]
e My mother wants to travel, but she doesn't know where. [ ]
f The barbecue is this afternoon. [ ]

1 _____ (you / buy) the meat and fish _____?
2 __Have you ever done__ (you / do) a sponsored swim?
3 _____ (she / be) abroad?
4 _____ (it / stop) raining _____?
5 _____ (she / find) her glasses _____?
6 _____ (anyone / make) him a cake _____?

5 Complete the quiz questions with *ever* and the present perfect form of the verbs in parentheses. Then answer the questions for you. Use *already*, *never*, or *yet*.

> There are lots of fun and creative ways to raise money for charity or to do something for your community. Which ones have you tried?

Have you ever cleaned up (clean up) a beach?
Yes, I have already cleaned up a beach. / No, I haven't cleaned up a beach yet. / No, I've never cleaned up a beach.

A _____ (wear) a red nose for a day?
_____
_____

B _____ (sing) in front of the whole school?
_____
_____

C _____ (have) a pajama party?
_____
_____

D _____ (paint) people's faces?
_____
_____

E _____ (dance) for twelve hours without stopping?
_____
_____

F _____ (organize) a big picnic?
_____
_____

G _____ (play) a musical instrument in the street?
_____
_____

H _____ (sell) things at a community yard sale?
_____
_____

6 Write true sentences about you, your family, and your friends. Use *never*.

Write about:

a a sport, game, or activity

| ~~play~~ | do |

My father has never played golf.
_____

b food

| eat | try |

_____
_____

c clothes and fashion

| wear | buy |

_____
_____

d places

| visit | see |

_____
_____

UNIT 8

VOCABULARY 2

make and do

1 Complete the phrases with *make* or *do*.

   make someone happy
   a _____ a decision
   b _____ charity work
   c _____ a mistake
   d _____ exercise
   e _____ someone a favor
   f _____ friends
   g _____ homework
   h _____ someone laugh
   i _____ nothing
   j _____ money
   k _____ your best

2 Match phrases from activity 1 with the pictures.

Happy birthday. This is for you.
That's fantastic! It's just what I wanted.

make someone happy

18 + 6 = 25.
No, that's wrong.
a _____

I'm doing this map for my geography project first, then I'm learning my French vocabulary.
b _____

I'm going for a run now. I run every day after school.
c _____

Yes, they're an amazing team. They probably will win, so you have to work very hard.
d _____

You don't need a winch. We'll help you.
e _____

3 Complete the sentences with phrases from activity 1. Use the correct form of *make* or *do*.

I love _doing nothing_ on Sunday evening before a busy week at school.

a Come on, hurry up. We need your answer. Please _____.

b I love those comedy shows on Channel 2. They're so funny. They always _____ me _____.

c She's at a new school and she hasn't _____ with anyone in her class yet.

d Top soccer players _____ a lot of _____. They can earn millions of dollars a year.

e She's a doctor, but, at the moment, she's _____ in a hospital abroad.

f I've _____ in the exercise, so I need to correct it.

GRAMMAR 2

Present Perfect: *for* and *since*

1 Circle the correct words.

I've known him **for** / **since** two years.
- **a** She's been here **for** / **since** four o'clock.
- **b** Gloria hasn't played tennis **for** / **since** March.
- **c** I haven't seen Georgia **for** / **since** years.
- **d** I've lived in Barcelona **for** / **since** I was born.
- **e** I've been at home **for** / **since** a week.
- **f** We've been friends **for** / **since** we were children.

2 Order the words to make sentences.

here / Monday / has / Jane / since / been
Jane has been here since Monday.

- **a** 2018 / has / in a bookstore / My sister / since / worked
  _____
- **b** since / haven't / the fire / been / They / at school
  _____
- **c** him / for / known / ages / I've
  _____
- **d** three / had / years / Anna / a motorcycle / for / has
  _____
- **e** eaten / since / She / with Harry / that awful meal / hasn't
  _____

3 Write questions with *How long …* Then answer using *for* or *since*.

you / live in Granada? (two years)
How long have you lived in Granada?
I've lived in Granada for two years.

- **a** you / have that laptop? (March)
  _____
  _____
- **b** that restaurant / be open? (two weeks)
  _____
  _____
- **c** she / work for that charity? (2018)
  _____
  _____
- **d** they / know each other? (they were two)
  _____
  _____
- **e** Luis / wear glasses? (two years)
  _____
  _____

4 Complete the email with the present perfect form of the verbs in parentheses. Circle *for* or *since*.

To: Anita
From: Daniel
Subject: Hi! :-)

Hi, Anita!
I'm sorry I ___haven't written___ (not write) to you **for** / **since** a long time. I **a** _____ (be) very busy **for** / **since** the beginning of term. I **b** _____ (join) the basketball team and we **c** _____ (have) three matches so far. I **d** _____ (not play) tennis **for** / **since** last summer because I **e** _____ (not have) time. I **f** _____ (not see) Rob **for** / **since** a very long time. I think he **g** _____ (go) to live in Brighton. **h** _____ (you / hear) from him? I **i** _____ (make) some really nice new friends at the drama club. We **j** _____ (write) a play together and we're acting in it next term. You must come and see it.
Bye for now,
Daniel

5 Write sentences about you, your family, and your friends. Use the present perfect with *for* or *since*.

I have been at this school for four years.
We have lived in our apartment since 2017.

- **a** _____ been _____.
- **b** _____ lived _____.
- **c** _____ had _____.
- **d** _____ known _____.
- **e** _____ studied _____.

UNIT 8

GRAMMAR CHECK

1 Read the text and circle the correct answers.

Since last March, we **a** ____ nearly 700 dollars for Médecins Sans Frontières. We are very pleased. And now we **b** ____ started to raise money for Oxfam too. So far, Carol **c** ____ organized a community yard sale. We **d** ____ had the sale yet, but some of us have **e** ____ a sponsored swim. We have **f** ____ a charity benefit concert, so maybe we can try that this year. At my school, the teachers and students have done charity work **g** ____ 2010. And we've sponsored a school **h** ____ three years. With our support, they have **i** ____ desks and a board for a new classroom. **j** ____ you ever done anything interesting to raise money?

	1	2	3
a	raising	(have raised)	were raising
b	have	did	were
c	did	was	has
d	haven't	didn't	couldn't
e	already did	already doing	already done
f	made never	ever made	never made
g	before	since	in
h	before	since	for
i	bought	buy	buying
j	Did	Have	Were

2 Listen and check your answers.

22))

LISTENING

1 Listen to two volunteers talking about their work for Clean Beaches. Circle the correct answers.

23))

  a The volunteers are cleaning **parks / beaches / roads**.

  b Maria Adams is a **teacher / student / secretary** at the community school.

  c They're finding **more garbage / less garbage / the same amount of garbage** this year.

  d Andy is a **student / teacher / office worker** at the school.

  e He arrived at **one o'clock / three thirty / nine thirty**.

  f He is volunteering because **he gets free lunch / the school makes him / he cares about the environment**.

2 Listen again and answer the questions.

23))

  a How many kilometers have they cleaned up so far?
  _____

  b When did the Clean Beaches campaign start?
  _____

  c How much less garbage are they finding this year?
  _____

  d What does Maria say about beaches in the state?
  _____

  e How many items were they picking up per kilometer last year?
  _____

  f How many items are they picking up per kilometer this year?
  _____

  g What has Andy picked up today?
  _____

  h How long has he been there?
  _____

  i What's the strangest thing he has found?
  _____
  _____

  j What are the fun activities at the end of the day?
  _____
  _____

EXTENSION

Circle the correct options to complete the text.

Our school has collected money for different charities **a since / for** five years now. We all really enjoy **b organizing / to organize** different fundraising activities. Last year, we **c made / have made** 3,000 dollars for the Red Cross with a big "Charity Day." We **d were selling / sold** different products on the community yard sale and washed cars. There **e were / was** also a pet show. It was the **f funniest / funnier** event of the day. While Peter Shepherd in Year 9 **g was showing / showed** his parrot to the judges, it started to say really bad words and the principal **h has got / got** very annoyed. He said the parrot was not polite **i enough for / enough to** win! This year we **j are organizing / organize** a benefit concert, a fashion show, and a karaoke. We haven't had a benefit concert **k since / for** 2018. And we've **l never did / never done** a fashion show before, although a fashion show isn't as **m interested / interesting** as a pet show. **n Have / Did** you ever done karaoke? I **o haven't / didn't** because I'm too frightened **p for singing / to sing** in public!

UNIT 8

VOCABULARY PLUS

Money

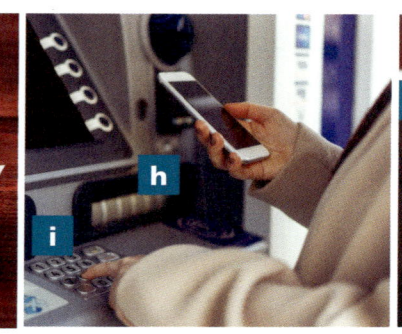

a _____
b _____
c _____
d _____
e _____
f _____
g _____
h _____
i _____
j _____

1 Label the pictures with the words in the box. Then listen and repeat.

ATM (automated teller machine)	pay by credit card
bills	pay in cash
check	PIN (personal identification number)
coin purse	tip
coins	wallet

2 Circle the correct options.

I've never had a 50 dollars **coin** / **bill**.

a "Waiter! Can we have the **check** / **tip**, please?" "Certainly."

b Someone stole my dad's **ATM** / **wallet** yesterday.

c I don't have enough bills. I'll pay **by credit card** / **in cash**.

d You shouldn't show anyone your **coin purse** / **PIN**.

e You can't get **coins** / **bills** from an ATM.

3 Read the definitions and write the correct words.

Men usually keep their bills in this.
___wallet___

a Women usually keep their coins in this. _____

b You can get money from here 24 hours a day. _____

c You leave this if you're happy with the service in a restaurant. _____

d If you pay with bills and coins, you do this. _____

e A piece of paper that shows you how much to pay in a restaurant. _____

4 Answer the questions for you. Write in full sentences. Use words from activity 1.

a Where do you keep your money?
_____
_____

b How do you usually pay in a store?
_____
_____

WORDLIST

PHONETIC CHART

VOWELS AND DIPHTHONGS

/ɪ/ pig	/e/ bread	/u/ lose	/aɪ/ I
/i/ she	/ɜr/ curly	/ə/ actor	/ɔɪ/ toy
/æ/ cat	/ɔ/ ball	/ʌ/ sunny	/aʊ/ mountain
/ɑ/ arm	/ʊ/ good	/eɪ/ USA	/oʊ/ boat

CONSONANTS

/p/ potato	/tʃ/ chair	/s/ Spain	/n/ newsstand
/b/ blue	/dʒ/ fridge	/z/ easy	/ŋ/ spring
/t/ taxi	/f/ finish	/ʃ/ shower	/l/ lake
/d/ drama	/v/ verb	/ʒ/ television	/r/ read
/k/ carrot	/θ/ bathroom	/h/ hi	/j/ yesterday
/g/ grandpa	/ð/ there	/m/ mouth	/w/ water

A

acoustic guitar (n) /əˈkustɪk gɪˈtɑr/
across (prep) /əˈkrɔs/
action-adventure (n) /ˈækʃ(ə)n ədˈventʃər/
actor (n) /ˈæktər/
advertise (v) /ˈædvərˌtaɪz/
advertisement (n) /ædˈvɜrtɪsmənt/
along (prep) /əˈlɔŋ/
already (adv) /ɔlˈredi/
also (adv) /ˈɔlsoʊ/
aluminum (n) /əˈlumɪnəm/
anniversary (n) /ˌænɪˈvɜrs(ə)ri/
annoy (v) /əˈnɔɪ/
annoyed (adj) /əˈnɔɪd/
annoying (adj) /əˈnɔɪɪŋ/
answer (v) /ˈænsər/
apartheid (n) /əˈpɑrtˌhaɪt/
appear (v) /əˈpɪr/
architect (n) /ˈɑrkɪˌtekt/
argue (v) /ˈɑrˌgju/
argument (n) /ˈɑrgjəmənt/
around (prep) /əˈraʊnd/
artist (n) /ˈɑrtɪst/
ask (v) /æsk/
ate (v) /eɪt/
athlete (n) /ˈæθˌlit/
ATM (automated teller machine) (n) /ˌeɪ ti ˈem/
autograph (n) /ˈɔtəˌgræf/
autumn (n) /ˈɔtəm/
avalanche (n) /ˈævəˌlæntʃ/
award (n) /əˈwɔrd/
away from (prep) /əˈweɪ frʌm/

B

bag (n) /bæg/
be (v) /bi/
be born (v) /bi bɔrn/
be going to /bi ˈgoʊɪŋ tu/

because (conj) /bɪˈkɔz/
began (v) /bɪˈgæn/
begin (v) /bɪˈgɪn/
bill (n) /bɪl/
biomedicine (n) /ˈbaɪoʊˌmedɪsɪn/
birth (n) /bɜrθ/
birthday celebration (n) /ˈbɜrθˌdeɪ ˌseləˈbreɪʃ(ə)n/
blind (adj) /blaɪnd/
blizzard (n) /ˈblɪzərd/
boots (n) /buts/
bore (v) /bɔr/
bored (adj) /bɔrd/
boring (adj) /ˈbɔrɪŋ/
bottle (n) /ˈbɑt(ə)l/
box (n) /bɑks/
box office (n) /bɑks ˈɔfɪs/
break (v) /breɪk/
bric-a-brac sale (n) /ˈbrɪkəˌbræk seɪl/
broken arm /ˈbroʊkən ɑrm/
bulletproof vest (n) /ˈbʊlɪtˌpruf vest/
buy a house /baɪ ə haʊs/

C

call (v) /kɔl/
can (n) /kæn/
cardboard (n) /ˈkɑrdˌbɔrd/
carton (n) /ˈkɑrt(ə)n/
cell phone (n) /sel foʊn/
chat (v) /tʃæt/
check (n) /tʃek/
chimpanzee (n) /ˌtʃɪmpænˈzi/
clean-tech (n) /klin tek/
cliff (n) /klɪf/
cloudy (adj) /ˈklaʊdi/
coast (n) /koʊst/
coat (n) /koʊt/
coin (n) /kɔɪn/
coin purse (n) /kɔɪn pɜrs/

WORDLIST

cold (n) /koʊld/
come (v) /kʌm/
compete (v) /kəmˈpit/
competition (n) /ˌkampəˈtɪʃ(ə)n/
computer (n) /kəmˈpjutər/
connect (v) /kəˈnekt/
connection (n) /kəˈnekʃ(ə)n/
construction worker (n) /kənˈstrʌkʃ(ə)n ˈwɜrkər/
contaminated water (n) /kənˈtæmɪˌneɪtəd ˈwɔtər/
cotton (n) /ˈkat(ə)n/
cough (n) /kɑf/
cow (n) /kaʊ/
crash (v) /kræʃ/
crocodile (n) /ˈkrɑkəˌdaɪl/
cut (v) /kʌt/
cycle (v) /ˈsaɪk(ə)l/
cyclone (n) /ˈsaɪˌkloʊn/

30))) **D**
death (n) /deθ/
decorate (v) /ˈdekəˌreɪt/
decoration (n) /ˌdekəˈreɪʃ(ə)n/
department store (n) /dɪˈpɑrtmənt stɔr/
develop (v) /dɪˈveləp/
development (n) /dɪˈveləpmənt/
die (v) /daɪ/
digital media (n) /ˈdɪdʒɪt(ə)l ˈmidiə/
director (n) /dɪˈrektər/
disease (n) /dɪˈziz/
disposable glove (n) /dɪˈspoʊzəb(ə)l glʌv/
divorce (n) /dɪˈvɔrs/
do a sponsored swim /du ə ˈspɑnsərd swɪm/
do charity work /du ˈtʃerəti wɜrk/
do exercise /du ˈeksərˌsaɪz/
do homework /du ˈhoʊmˌwɜrk/
do nothing /du ˈnʌθɪŋ/
do someone a favor /du ˈsʌmwʌn ə ˈfeɪvər/
do your best /du jʊr best/
doctor (n) /ˈdɑktər/
dolphin (n) /ˈdɑlfɪn/
dot-com company (n) /ˌdɑtˈkɑm ˈkʌmpəni/
down (prep) /daʊn/
dress (n) /dres/
drive (v) /draɪv/
drown (v) /draʊn/
drums (n) /drʌmz/
dry (adj) /draɪ/

31))) **E**
earache (n) /ˈɪrˌeɪk/
earmuffs (n) /ˈɪrˌmʌfs/
earring (n) /ˈɪrɪŋ/
educate (v) /ˈedʒəˌkeɪt/
education (n) /ˌedʒəˈkeɪʃ(ə)n/
electric bass (n) /ɪˈlektrɪk beɪs/
electric guitar (n) /ɪˈlektrɪk gɪˈtɑr/
elephant (n) /ˈeləfənt/
engagement (n) /ɪnˈgeɪdʒmənt/

engineer (n) /ˌendʒɪˈnɪr/
enjoy (v) /ɪnˈdʒɔɪ/
enjoyment (n) /ɪnˈdʒɔɪmənt/
equip (v) /ɪˈkwɪp/
escape (v) /ɪˈskeɪp/
ever (adv) /ˈevər/
excite (v) /ɪkˈsaɪt/
excited (adj) /ɪkˈsaɪtəd/
excitement (n) /ɪkˈsaɪtmənt/
exciting (adj) /ɪkˈsaɪtɪŋ/

32))) **F**
face mask (n) /feɪs mæsk/
factory (n) /ˈfækt(ə)ri/
feel (v) /fil/
fell (v) /fel/
film a scene /fɪlm ə sin/
financial service (n) /fɪˈnænʃ(ə)l ˈsɜrvɪs/
flew (v) /flu/
flute (n) /flut/
for (prep / conj) /fɔr/
found (v) /faʊnd/
friendship (n) /ˈfren(d)ʃɪp/
frighten (v) /ˈfraɪt(ə)n/
frightened (adj) /ˈfraɪt(ə)nd/
frightening (adj) /ˈfraɪt(ə)nɪŋ/
fundraising (n) /ˈfʌndˌreɪzɪŋ/

33))) **G**
games (n) /geɪmz/
garage (n) /gəˈrɑʒ/
garage sale (n) /gəˈrɑʒ seɪl/
get (v) /get/
get a job /get ə dʒɑb/
get married /get ˈmerid/
give (v) /gɪv/
glass (n) /glæs/
glove (n) /glʌv/
go (v) /goʊ/
go to /goʊ tu /
go to college /goʊ tu ˈkɑlɪdʒ/
Good Deeds Day (n) /gʊd dids deɪ/
Goodwill Ambassador (n) /gʊdˈwɪl æmˈbæsədər/
got (v) /gɑt/
got stuck /gɑt stʌk/
grow (v) /groʊ/

34))) **H**
hailstorm (n) /ˈheɪlˌstɔrm/
happen (v) /ˈhæpən/
have children /hæv ˈtʃɪldrən/
headache (n) /ˈhedˌeɪk/
hear (v) /hɪr/
heat wave (n) /hit weɪv/
helmet (n) /ˈhelmət/
hide (v) /haɪd/
high drama (n) /haɪ ˈdrɑmə/
high school (n) /haɪ skul/

high visibility jacket (n) /ˌhaɪ vɪzəˈbɪləti ˈdʒækət/
hold (v) /hoʊld/
Hollywood blockbuster (n) /ˈhaliˌwʊd ˈblɑkˌbʌstər/
hospital (n) /ˈhɑspɪt(ə)l/
hot (adj) /hɑt/
how long /haʊ lɔŋ/

35 I

inform (v) /ɪnˈfɔrm/
information (n) /ˌɪnfərˈmeɪʃ(ə)n/
insect bite (n) /ˈɪnˌsekt baɪt/
inspector (n) /ɪnˈspektər/
interest (n) /ˈɪntrəst/
interested (adj) /ˈɪntrəstɪd/
interesting (adj) /ˈɪntrəstɪŋ/
internet browser (n) /ˈɪntərˌnet ˈbraʊzər/
into (prep) /ˈɪntu/
introduce (v) /ˌɪntrəˈdus/
invite (v) /ɪnˈvaɪt/

36 J

jacket (n) /ˈdʒækət/
Jamaica (n) /dʒəˈmeɪkə/
jar (n) /dʒɑr/
jeans (n) /dʒinz/
journalist (n) /ˈdʒɜrn(ə)lɪst/
just (adv) /dʒʌst/

37 L

lawyer (n) /ˈlɔjər/
learn to drive /lɜrn tu draɪv/
leave home /liv hoʊm/
leave school /liv skul/
leopard (n) /ˈlepərd/
lie (v) /laɪ/
lion (n) /ˈlaɪən/
listen (v) /ˈlɪs(ə)n/
live (v) /lɪv/
look (v) /lʊk/
lost (v) /lɔst/
love (v) /lʌv/

38 M

make (v) /meɪk/
make a decision /meɪk ə dɪˈsɪʒ(ə)n/
make a mistake /meɪk ə mɪˈsteɪk/
make friends /meɪk frendz/
make money /meɪk ˈmʌni/
make someone happy /meɪk ˈsʌmwʌn ˈhæpi/
make someone laugh /meɪk ˈsʌmwʌn læf/
manage (v) /ˈmænɪdʒ/
Maori (n) /ˈmaʊri/
market opportunity (n) /ˈmɑrkət ˌɑpərˈtunəti/
meanwhile (adv) /ˈminˌwaɪl/
mechanic (n) /məˈkænɪk/
medical field (n) /ˈmedɪk(ə)l fild/
metal (n) /ˈmet(ə)l/
mild (adj) /maɪld/

monkey (n) /ˈmʌŋki/
mountain range (n) /ˈmaʊnt(ə)n reɪndʒ/
movie premiere (n) /ˈmuvi prɪˈmɪr/
movie star (n) /ˈmuvi stɑr/
moviemaker (n) /ˈmuviˌmeɪkər/
moviemaking (n) /ˈmuviˌmeɪkɪŋ/
multiplex movie theater (n) /ˈmʌltɪˌpleks ˈmuvi ˈθiətər/
must (v) /mʌst/

39 N

notice (v) /ˈnoʊtɪs/
nurse (n) /nɜrs/

40 O

ocean (n) /ˈoʊʃ(ə)n/
office (n) /ˈɔfɪs/
online (adj) /ˈɑnˌlaɪn/
open (v) /ˈoʊpən/
orangutan (n) /ɔˈræŋəˌtæn/
out of (prep) /aʊt əv/
over (prep) /ˈoʊvər/
overall (n) /ˈoʊvərˌɔl/

41 P

panda (n) /ˈpændə/
paper (n) /ˈpeɪpər/
pass (v) /pæs/
pay by credit card /peɪ baɪ ˈkredɪt kɑrd/
pay in cash /peɪ ɪn kæʃ/
percussion (n) /pərˈkʌʃ(ə)n/
phone (n) /foʊn/
piano (n) /piˈænoʊ/
PIN (n) /pɪn/
plot (n) /plɑt/
plug (v) /plʌg/
polar bear (n) /ˈpoʊlər ber/
police officer (n) /pəˈlis ˈɔfɪsər/
police station (n) /pəˈlis ˈsteɪʃ(ə)n/
politician (n) /ˌpɑləˈtɪʃ(ə)n/
pond (n) /pɑnd/
poor sanitation (n) /pʊr ˌsænɪˈteɪʃ(ə)n/
popcorn (n) /ˈpɑpˌkɔrn/
possess (v) /pəˈzes/
possession (n) /pəˈzeʃ(ə)n/
post a comment /poʊst ə ˈkɑˌment/
predict (v) /prɪˈdɪkt/
prediction (n) /prɪˈdɪkʃ(ə)n/
prepare (v) /prɪˈper/
producer (n) /prəˈdusər/
put (v) /pʊt/

42 Q

queue (n) /kju/

43 R

rain boot (n) /reɪn but/
rainy (adj) /ˈreɪni/
read an e-book /rid æn i-bʊk/

WORDLIST

researcher (n) /rɪˈsɜrtʃər/
recognize (v) /ˈrekəɡˌnaɪz/
recycle (v) /riˈsaɪk(ə)l/
reduce (v) rɪˈdus/
refer (v) /rɪˈfɜr/
release a movie /rɪˈlis ə ˈmuvi/
retirement (n) /rɪˈtaɪrmənt/
reuse (v) /ˌriˈjuz/
rhinoceros (n) /raɪˈnɑsərəs/
Royal Bengal Tiger (n) /ˈrɔɪəl ˈbeŋɡəl ˈtaɪɡər/

44))) S

safety glasses (n) /ˈseɪfti ˈɡlɑsəz/
sandal (n) /ˈsænd(ə)l/
saxophone (n) /ˈsæksəˌfoʊn/
scan a picture /skæn ə ˈpɪktʃər/
scarf (n) /skɑrf/
science fiction (n) /ˈsaɪəns ˈfɪkʃ(ə)n/
scientist (n) /ˈsaɪəntɪst/
script (n) /skrɪpt/
seat (n) /sit/
see (v) /si/
shark attack (n) /ʃɑrk əˈtæk/
shirt (n) /ʃɜrt/
shorts (n) /ʃɔrts/
should (v) /ʃʊd/
show (v) /ʃoʊ/
sick (adj) /sɪk/
since (adv / conj / prep) /sɪns/
Singapore (n) /ˈsɪŋəˌpɔr/
skirt (n) /skɜrt/
slipper (n) /ˈslɪpər/
smart TV (n) /smɑrt ˌti ˈvi/
smile (v) /smaɪl/
snake (n) /sneɪk/
sneakers (n) /ˈsnikərz/
snowy (adj) /ˈsnoʊi/
so (adv / conj) /soʊ/
soft drink (n) /sɔft drɪŋk/
soon (adv) /sun/
sore throat (n) /sɔr θroʊt/
soundtrack (n) /ˈsaʊn(d)ˌtræk/
South Africa (n) /saʊθ ˈæfrɪkə/
special effects (n) /ˈspeʃ(ə)l ɪˈfekts/
sports club (n) /spɔrts klʌb/
spring (n) /sprɪŋ/
star in a movie /stɑr ɪn ə ˈmuvi/
start school /stɑrt skul/
stay (v) /steɪ/
stomachache (n) /ˈstʌmək eɪk/
stop (v) /stɑp/
store (v) /stɔr/
stormy (adj) /ˈstɔrmi/
stream (n) /strim/
study (v) /ˈstʌdi/
study abroad (n) /ˈstʌdi əˈbrɔd/
stunt (n) /stʌnt/

suddenly (adv) /ˈsʌd(ə)nli/
suggest (v) /səɡˈdʒest/
suggestion (n) /səɡˈdʒestʃ(ə)n/
summer (n) /ˈsʌmər/
sun hat (n) /sʌn hæt/
sunny (adj) /ˈsʌni/
surf (v) /sɜrf/
surgeon (n) /ˈsɜrdʒən/
surprise (v) /sərˈpraɪz/
surprised (adj) /sərˈpraɪzd/
surprising (adj) /sərˈpraɪzɪŋ/
survive (v) /sərˈvaɪv/
swam (v) /swæm/
sweater (n) /ˈswetər/
swim (v) /swɪm/

45))) T

take (v) /teɪk/
talk (v) /tɔk/
teacher (n) /ˈtitʃər/
technician (n) /tekˈnɪʃ(ə)n/
technology sector (n) /tekˈnɑlədʒi ˈsektər/
tell (v) /tel/
temperature (n) /ˈtemp(ə)rəˌtʃʊr/
theater (n) /ˈθiətər/
then (adj / adv) /ðen/
think (v) /θɪŋk/
thunderstorm (n) /ˈθʌndərˌstɔrm/
ticket (n) /ˈtɪkɪt/
tie (n) /taɪ/
tiger (n) /ˈtaɪɡər/
tip (n) /tɪp/
tire (v) /ˈtaɪr/
tired (adj) /ˈtaɪrd/
tiring (adj) /ˈtaɪrɪŋ/
tomorrow (adv) /təˈmɔroʊ/
too (adv) /tu/
took (v) /tʊk/
towards (prep) /tɔrdz/
train to be a /treɪn tu bi ə/
Trinidad and Tobago (n) /ˈtrɪnɪˌdæd ænd təˈbeɪɡoʊ/
trumpet (n) /ˈtrʌmpət/
try (v) /traɪ/
T-shirt (n) /ti-ʃɜrt/
turtle (n) /ˈtɜrt(ə)l/

46))) U

umbrella (n) /ʌmˈbrelə/
under (prep) /ˈʌndər/
up (prep) /ʌp/
upload (v) /ˈʌpˌloʊd/
URL (n) /ˌju ɑr ˈel/
use (v) /juz/

47))) V

valley (n) /ˈvæli/
vet (n) /vet/

video game (n) /ˈvɪdioʊ ɡeɪm/
violin (n) /ˌvaɪəˈlɪn/
visor (n) /ˈvaɪzər/

48))) **W**

wait (v) /weɪt/
want (v) /wɑnt/
warm (adj) /wɔrm/
was (v) /wɑz/
wash cars /wɑʃ kɑrz/
water molecule (n) /ˈwɔtər ˈmɑləˌkjul/
water service (n) /ˈwɔtər ˈsɜrvɪs/
waterproof (n) /ˈwɔtərˌpruf/
waterproof jacket (n) /ˈwɔtərˌpruf ˈdʒækət/
wave (n) /weɪv/
wear (v) /wer/
web page (n) /ˈweb peɪdʒ/
website (n) /ˈwebˌsaɪt/
wedding (n) /ˈwedɪŋ/
were (v) /wɜr/

wet (adj) /wet/
while (conj) /waɪl/
wildfire (n) /ˈwaɪldˌfaɪr/
will (v) /wɪl/
win an award /wɪn æn əˈwɔrd/
windy (adj) /ˈwɪndi/
winter (n) /ˈwɪntər/
wool (n) /wʊl/
work (v) /wɜrk/
work with children /wɜrk wɪð ˈtʃɪldrən/
World Water Day (n) /wɜrld ˈwɔtər deɪ/
World Wide Web (n) /wɜrld waɪd web/
worried (adj) /ˈwʌrid/
worry (v) /ˈwʌri/
worrying (adj) /ˈwʌriɪŋ/
write (v) /raɪt/

49))) **Y**

yard sale (n) /jɑrd seɪl/
yet (adv) /jet/

2022 © Macmillan Education Brasil

Based on *InstaEnglish* and *Motivate*
© Macmillan Education Brasil 2019 and Macmillan Education Limited 2013
Written by Emma Heyderman, Fiona Mauchline, Patrick Howarth, Patricia Reilly and Olivia Johnston
Grammar, *Speaking*, and *Culture* pages adapted by Gisele Marçon Bastos Périgo and Thelma de Carvalho Guimarães
Vocabulary, *Reading*, and *Writing* pages adapted by Thelma de Carvalho Guimarães
Digital Literacy and *Global Citizenship* pages created by Thelma de Carvalho Guimarães

Director of Languages Brazil: Patricia Souza De Luccia
Publishing Manager and Field Researcher: Patricia Muradas
Content Creation Coordinator: Cristina do Vale
Art Coordinator: Jean Aranha
Lead Editors: Gabriel França, Roberta Somera
Content Editors: Ana Beatriz da Costa Moreira, Gabriel França, Roberta Somera, Tatiana Martins Santana
Digital Editors: Deborah Stafussi, Elaine Lins
Editorial Assistant: Carolina Araújo de Melo, Daniela Alves
Editorial Intern: Pedro Improta
Art Assistant: Jacqueline Alves
Art Intern: Victor Augusto Amorim
Editorial Apprentice: Beatriz Jacinto
Graphic Production: Alexandra L. S. de Carvalho, Thais Mendes P. Galvão
Proofreaders: Ana Lúcia Mendes Reis, Cátia de Almeida, Edward Willson, Rhiannon Ball
Design Concept: Martha Tadaieski
Page Makeup: Figurattiva Editorial
Photo Research: Marcia Sato
Illustrations: Bruna Assis
Image Processing: Jacqueline Alves, Jean Aranha, Victor Augusto Amorim
Extra Interactive Activities Content Development: Daniela Alves
Cover Concept: Jean Aranha
Cover photography: BartekSzewczyk/iStockphoto/Getty Images
Audio: Argila
Video: Desenredo

Reproduction prohibited. Penal Code Article 184 and Law number 9.610 of February 19, 1998.

We would like to dedicate this book to teachers all over Brazil. We would also like to thank our clients and teachers who have helped us make this book better with their many rich contributions and feedback straight from the classroom!

The authors, adaptor and publishers would like to thank the following for permission to reproduce the photographic material:
p. 88: Imgorthand/iStockphoto/Getty Images. p. 90: Highwaystarz-Photography/iStockphoto/Getty Images; Delmaine Donson/iStockphoto/Getty Images; Drazen Zigic/iStockphoto/Getty Images; gchutka/iStockphoto/Getty Images; Marina Cavusoglu/iStockphoto/Getty Images; USGirl/iStockphoto/Getty Images. p. 91: PeopleImages/iStockphoto/Getty Images; DisobeyArt/iStockphoto/Getty Images; ozgurcankaya/iStockphoto/Getty Images; Caiaimage/Agnieszka Wozniak/iStockphoto/Getty Images. p. 92: JuiceBros/iStockphoto/Getty Images. p. 93: Juanmonino/iStockphoto/Getty Images. p. 94: LightFieldStudios/iStockphoto/Getty Images. p. 95: RossHelen/iStockphoto/Getty Images; Wavebreakmedia/iStockphoto/Getty Images; GaudiLab/iStockphoto/Getty Images. p. 96: sihuo0860371/iStockphoto/Getty Images; EdnaM/iStockphoto/Getty Images; Stefan Rotter/iStockphoto/Getty Images; GeorgePeters/iStockphoto/Getty Images; perets/iStockphoto/Getty Images; megaflopp/iStockphoto/Getty Images; by_nicholas/iStockphoto/Getty Images; tifonimages/iStockphoto/Getty Images; AlexMaster/iStockphoto/Getty Images; leezsnow/iStockphoto/Getty Images; LAUDISENO/iStockphoto/Getty Images; millann/iStockphoto/Getty Images; Olga Zakharova/iStockphoto/Getty Images; master1305/iStockphoto/Getty Images; Laures/iStockphoto/Getty Images. p. 99: wellesenterprises/iStockphoto/Getty Images; JasonDoiy/iStockphoto/Getty Images. p. 101: MesquitaFMS/iStockphoto/Getty Images; Ivan Pantic/iStockphoto/Getty Images. p. 102: FatCamera/iStockphoto/Getty Images. p. 103: stnazkul/iStockphoto/Getty Images; bernardbodo/iStockphoto/Getty Images; Cecilie_Arcurs/iStockphoto/Getty Images; FG Trade/iStockphoto/Getty Images; SeventyFour/iStockphoto/Getty Images; FatCamera/iStockphoto/Getty Images; Prostock-Studio/iStockphoto/Getty Images; kali9/iStockphoto/Getty Images; FG Trade/iStockphoto/Getty Images; supersizer/iStockphoto/Getty Images; WinnieVinzence/iStockphoto/Getty Images; Vasyl Dolmatov/iStockphoto/Getty Images; Igor Alecsander/iStockphoto/Getty Images; Tim Allen/iStockphoto/Getty Images; jane/iStockphoto/Getty Images; piola666/iStockphoto/Getty Images; FangXiaNuo/iStockphoto/Getty Images; shironosov/iStockphoto/Getty Images; Fred_Pinheiro/iStockphoto/Getty Images; joka2000/iStockphoto/Getty Images; Vladimir Vladimirov/iStockphoto/Getty Images; Pom669/iStockphoto/Getty Images; urbazon/iStockphoto/Getty Images. p. 104: waltkowalski/iStockphoto/Getty Images. p. 106: Future-Image/ZUMA Press/Imageplus; gorodenkoff/iStockphoto/Getty Images; MediaProduction/iStockphoto/Getty Images; Erdark/iStockphoto/Getty Images; guruXOOX/iStockphoto/Getty Images. p. 107: IAM-photography/iStockphoto/Getty Images. p. 108: filipefrazao/iStockphoto/Getty Images. p. 109: ChubarovY/iStockphoto/Getty Images. p. 110: nyul/iStockphoto/Getty Images; Dimension Films/Troublemaker Studios/Spy Kids 4 SPV; New Line Cinema/Walden Media; Pixar Animation Studios/Walt Disney Pictures. p. 111: worldofvector/iStockphoto/Getty Images; Lisa O'Connor/ZUMA Press/Imageplus. p. 112: Vladimir Vladimirov/iStockphoto/Getty Images; apomares/iStockphoto/Getty Images; Imagesbybarbara/iStockphoto/Getty Images; guruXOOX/iStockphoto/Getty Images. p. 113: JulyProkopiv/iStockphoto/Getty Images. p. 114: thenatchdl/iStockphoto/Getty Images; PeopleImages/iStockphoto/Getty Images; Walt Disney Studios Motion Pictures/Photofest/Easypix Brasil. p. 117: franckreporter/iStockphoto/Getty Images; Halfpoint/iStockphoto/Getty Images. p. 118: anttohoho/iStockphoto/Getty Images. p. 119: gorodenkoff/iStockphoto/Getty Images; guruXOOX/iStockphoto/Getty Images; Future-Image/ZUMA Press/Imageplus; fizkes/iStockphoto/Getty Images; pomphotomine/iStockphoto/Getty Images; PaoloScarlata/iStockphoto/Getty Images; MediaProduction/iStockphoto/Getty Images; Erdark/iStockphoto/Getty Images; brightstars/iStockphoto/Getty Images; Devrimb/iStockphoto/Getty Images; gorodenkoff/iStockphoto/Getty Images; IAM-photography/iStockphoto/Getty Images; visual7/iStockphoto/Getty Images; mbolina/iStockphoto/Getty Images; grinvalds/iStockphoto/Getty Images; NicolasMcComber/iStockphoto/Getty Images; master1305/iStockphoto/Getty Images; pixelfit/iStockphoto/Getty Images; nortonrsx/iStockphoto/Getty Images; ArtRachen01/iStockphoto/Getty Images; SDI Productions/iStockphoto/Getty Images; pixelfit/iStockphoto/Getty Images; dpmike/iStockphoto/Getty Images; evgenyatamanenko/iStockphoto/Getty Images; Pekic/iStockphoto/Getty Images; Ivan-balvan/iStockphoto/Getty Images; nullplus/iStockphoto/Getty Images; insta_photos/iStockphoto/Getty Images. p. 120: master1305/iStockphoto/Getty Images; sizsus/iStockphoto/Getty Images; SeventyFour/iStockphoto/Getty Images. p. 121: Pom669/iStockphoto/Getty Images; vzphotos/iStockphoto/Getty Images; BrianAJackson/iStockphoto/Getty Images. p. 125: Hanna Siamashka/iStockphoto/Getty Images. p. 126: shironosov/iStockphoto/Getty Images. p. 128: philipimage/iStockphoto/Getty Images; JoeLena/iStockphoto/Getty Images; WichienTep/iStockphoto/Getty Images; Lebazele/iStockphoto/Getty Images; artisteer/iStockphoto/Getty Images; pepifoto/iStockphoto/Getty Images; photooiasson/iStockphoto/Getty Images; amriphoto/iStockphoto/Getty Images; Muhammad Rizqi DPM/iStockphoto/Getty Images; alenkadr/iStockphoto/Getty Images; MediaProduction/iStockphoto/Getty Images; ptasha/iStockphoto/Getty Images; Thomas-Soellner/iStockphoto/Getty Images. p. 129: SolStock/iStockphoto/Getty Images; Suzi Media Production/iStockphoto/Getty Images; Arkadiusz Warguła/iStockphoto/Getty Images. p. 131: Wavebreakmedia/iStockphoto/Getty Images; kali9/iStockphoto/Getty Images. p. 132: Grandbrothers/iStockphoto/Getty Images; littleny/iStockphoto/Getty Images; Wavebreakmedia/iStockphoto/Getty Images. p. 133: Tomwang112/iStockphoto/Getty Images; Pley/iStockphoto/Getty Images; Jakub Dvorak/iStockphoto/Getty Images. p. 134: Ondrej Prosicky/iStockphoto/Getty Images; Alatom/iStockphoto/Getty Images; lemga/iStockphoto/Getty Images; UrmasPhotoCom/iStockphoto/Getty Images; na9/iStockphoto/Getty Images. p 135: Byronsdad/iStockphoto/Getty Images; Yuri_Arcurs/iStockphoto/Getty Images; pkline/iStockphoto/Getty Images; USO/iStockphoto/Getty Images; Kativ/iStockphoto/Getty Images. p. 136: max-kegfire/iStockphoto/Getty Images; Adrian Boot/Retna/Photoshot/UPPA/ZUMA PRESS/Imageplus. p. 137: Catherine Scotton/iStockphoto/Getty Images; RonTech2000/iStockphoto/Getty Images. p. 139: KeithSzafranski/iStockphoto/Getty Images. p. 140 eROMAZe/iStockphoto/Getty Images. p. 141: philipimage/iStockphoto/Getty Images; pepifoto/iStockphoto/Getty Images; WichienTep/iStockphoto/Getty Images; JoeLena/iStockphoto/Getty Images; Lebazele/iStockphoto/Getty Images; olm26250/iStockphoto/Getty Images; MediaProduction/iStockphoto/Getty Images; amriphoto/iStockphoto/Getty Images; Eivaisla/iStockphoto/Getty Images; alenkadr/iStockphoto/Getty Images; YinYang/iStockphoto/Getty Images; artisteer/iStockphoto/Getty Images; arkstart/iStockphoto/Getty Images; Muhammad Rizqi DPM/iStockphoto/Getty Images; slowmotiongli/iStockphoto/Getty Images; Ondrej Prosicky/iStockphoto/Getty Images; Luis Lima Jr/iStockphoto/Getty Images; Freder/iStockphoto/Getty Images; Alatom/iStockphoto/Getty Images; pkline/iStockphoto/Getty Images; Yuri_Arcurs/iStockphoto/Getty Images; DikkyOesin/iStockphoto/Getty Images; Kativ/iStockphoto/Getty Images; feel4nature/iStockphoto/Getty Images. p. 142: RyanJLane/iStockphoto/Getty Images. p. 144: RichLegg/iStockphoto/Getty Images; davidf/iStockphoto/Getty Images; Halfpoint/iStockphoto/Getty Images; FangXiaNuo/iStockphoto/Getty Images; bojanstory/iStockphoto/Getty Images. p. 145: Neeraj Kumar/iStockphoto/Getty Images. p. 147 Yevhenii Dubinko/iStockphoto/Getty Images. p. 148: mixetto/iStockphoto/Getty Images; Beeldbewerking/iStockphoto/Getty Images; erkan gozcan/iStockphoto/Getty Images; whitemay/iStockphoto/Getty Images. p. 149: Elliott & Fry/National Portrait Gallery; hadynyah/iStockphoto/Getty Images. p. 150: Drazen_/iStockphoto/Getty Images; Chris Pizzello / AP Photo / Imageplus; Richard Drew / AP Photo / Imageplus; James Diddick / Globe Photos / ZUMA Press / Imageplus; Dan Steinberg / Swiffer / AP Photo / Imageplus; Christophe Ena / AP Photo / Imageplus; Christopher Victorio / imageSPACE / MediaPunch / IPX / AP Photo / Imageplus; Ian West / PA Wire / ZUMA Press / Imageplus; Imaginechina / AP Photo / Imageplus. p. 152: SDI Productions/iStockphoto/Getty Images. p. 155: Wavebreakmedia/iStockphoto/Getty Images. p. 156: FangXiaNuo/iStockphoto/Getty Images. p. 157: GoodLifeStudio/iStockphoto/Getty Images; Halfpoint/iStockphoto/Getty Images; bojanstory/iStockphoto/Getty Images; davidf/iStockphoto/Getty Images; Razvan/iStockphoto/Getty Images; RichLegg/iStockphoto/Getty Images; FangXiaNuo/iStockphoto/Getty Images; DLMcK/iStockphoto/Getty Images; Pattanaphong Khuankaew/iStockphoto/Getty Images; fizkes/iStockphoto/Getty Images; monkeybusinessimages/iStockphoto/Getty Images; Xesai/iStockphoto/Getty Images; LightFieldStudios/iStockphoto/Getty Images; JohnnyGreig/iStockphoto/Getty Images; Halfpoint/iStockphoto/Getty Images; Photodjo/iStockphoto/Getty Images; arieliona/iStockphoto/Getty Images; NataBene/iStockphoto/Getty Images; Highwaystarz-Photography/iStockphoto/Getty Images; SDI Productions/iStockphoto/Getty Images. p. 158: Jovanmandic/iStockphoto/Getty Images; pkline/iStockphoto/Getty Images; skynesher/iStockphoto/Getty Images; LanaStock/iStockphoto/Getty Images; karelnoppe/iStockphoto/Getty Images; prpicturesproduction/iStockphoto/Getty Images; Yuri_Arcurs/iStockphoto/Getty Images; da-kuk/iStockphoto/Getty Images; Makidotvn/iStockphoto/Getty Images. p. 159: FG Trade/iStockphoto/Getty Images; MediaProduction/iStockphoto/Getty Images; Ondrej Prosicky/iStockphoto/Getty Images; artisteer/iStockphoto/Getty Images; OlafSpeier/iStockphoto/Getty Images; AntonioGuillem/iStockphoto/Getty Images; gojak/iStockphoto/Getty Images; Chainarong Prasertthai/iStockphoto/Getty Images; Richard Villalonundefined undefined/iStockphoto/Getty Images. p. 162: artbesouro/iStockphoto/Getty Images. p. 164: adventtr/iStockphoto/Getty Images; adekvat/iStockphoto/Getty Images; Turkan Rahimli/iStockphoto/Getty Images; VectorPocket/iStockphoto/Getty Images; mushakesa/iStockphoto/Getty Images; balzbalz/iStockphoto/Getty Images; peanutpie/iStockphoto/Getty Images; Turkan Rahimli/iStockphoto/Getty Images. p. 202: kazuma seki/iStockphoto/Getty Images; Satoshi-K/iStockphoto/Getty Images; Courtney Hale/iStockphoto/Getty Images; kkshepel/iStockphoto/Getty Images; FG Trade/iStockphoto/Getty Images; XiXinXing/iStockphoto/Getty Images; petekarici/iStockphoto/Getty Images; skynesher/iStockphoto/Getty Images; BartCo/iStockphoto/Getty Images; FatCamera/iStockphoto/Getty Images. p. 203: PeopleImages/iStockphoto/Getty Images; JohnnyGreig/iStockphoto/Getty Images; NKS_Imagery/iStockphoto/Getty Images; Inside Creative House/iStockphoto/Getty Images; Delmaine Donson/iStockphoto/Getty Images; EmirMemedovski/iStockphoto/Getty Images. p. 204: krblokhin/iStockphoto/Getty Images. p. 206: simonkr/iStockphoto/Getty Images. p. 207: fizkes/iStockphoto/Getty Images; Image Source/iStockphoto/Getty Images. p. 208: AmandaLewis/iStockphoto/Getty Images; GeorgiosArt/iStockphoto/Getty Images; Macmillan. p. 211: SCStock/iStockphoto/Getty Images. p. 212: cokada/iStockphoto/Getty Images. p. 214: NicoElNino/iStockphoto/Getty Images. p. 215: Grafissimo/iStockphoto/Getty Images. p. 216: MarsBars/iStockphoto/Getty Images; Warner Bros; Selznick International Pictures/Metro-Goldwyn-Mayer (MGM). p. 217: NicolasMcComber/iStockphoto/Getty Images; RgStudio/iStockphoto/Getty Images; danr13/iStockphoto/Getty Images; tifonimages/iStockphoto/Getty Images; Caiaimage/Tom Merton/iStockphoto/Getty Images; Paul Bradbury/iStockphoto/Getty Images; Paramount Pictures/Skydance Media/Jerry Bruckheimer Films/Don Simpson/Jerry Bruckheimer Films. p. 218: PeopleImages/iStockphoto/Getty Images; LanaStock/iStockphoto/Getty Images. p. 219: PeopleImages/iStockphoto/Getty Images; Bicho_raro/iStockphoto/Getty Images; AJ_Watt/iStockphoto/Getty Images; narxx/iStockphoto/Getty Images; PeopleImages/iStockphoto/Getty Images; Oksana Semak/iStockphoto/Getty Images. p. 220: Stígur Már Karlsson /Heimsmyndir/iStockphoto/Getty Images; Donhype/iStockphoto/Getty Images. p. 221: DamianKuzdak/iStockphoto/Getty Images; guenterguni/iStockphoto/Getty Images; KenCanning/iStockphoto/Getty Images; JasonPrince/iStockphoto/Getty Images; Hung_Chung_Chih/iStockphoto/Getty Images; Mario_Hoppmann/iStockphoto/Getty Images; eROMAZe/iStockphoto/Getty Images; Freder/iStockphoto/Getty Images; richcarey/iStockphoto/Getty Images; skynesher/iStockphoto/Getty Images. p. 222: primeimages/iStockphoto/Getty Images. p. 223: Rawpixel/iStockphoto/Getty Images; Markus Frenzel/iStockphoto/Getty Images. p. 224: FortyFour Studios/Pixar Animation Studios/Walt Disney Pictures; Tya H. Kottler/iStockphoto/Getty Images. p. 226: Pavel1964/iStockphoto/Getty Images; Camrocker/iStockphoto/Getty Images; monkeybusinessimages/iStockphoto/Getty Images; miodrag ignjatovic/iStockphoto/Getty Images; vejaa/iStockphoto/Getty Images. p. 227: David Sacks/iStockphoto/Getty Images. p. 229: TolikoffPhotography/iStockphoto/Getty Images; Image Source/iStockphoto/Getty Images; AndreaObzerova/iStockphoto/Getty Images; DimaBerkut/iStockphoto/Getty Images. p. 229: svetikd/iStockphoto/Getty Images; skynesher/iStockphoto/Getty Images; AleksandarGeorgiev/iStockphoto/Getty Images; FG Trade/iStockphoto/Getty Images; Liudmila Chernetska/iStockphoto/Getty Images; monkeybusinessimages/iStockphoto/Getty Images. p. 130: Intpro/iStockphoto/Getty Images. p. 231:

Karl-Hendrik Tittel/iStockphoto/Getty Images. p. 233: EmirMemedovski/iStockphoto/Getty Images; LukaTDB/iStockphoto/Getty Images; imagestock/iStockphoto/Getty Images; perets/iStockphoto/Getty Images; bibikoff/iStockphoto/Getty Images; VTT Studio/iStockphoto/Getty Images; Oleg Chumakov/iStockphoto/Getty Images; hsyncoban/iStockphoto/Getty Images.

```
Dados Internacionais de Catalogação na Publicação (CIP)
    (BENITEZ Catalogação Ass. Editorial, MS, Brasil)

I48    InstaEnglish 2nd edition level 2 student's
2.ed.     book and workbook : SPLIT B / Emma
          Heyderman...[et al.]. - 2.ed. -
          São Paulo : Macmillan Education do
          Brasil, 2023.
          128 p.; il.; 21 x 29,7 cm.

          Outros autores: Fiona Mauchline, Patrick
       Howarth, Patricia Reilly, Olivia Johnston.
          ISBN 978-65-5752-293-6

          1. Língua inglesa (Ensino fundamental).
       I. Mauchline, Fiona. II. Howarth, Patrick.
       III. Reilly, Patricia. IV. Johnston, Olivia.
05-2023/40                        CDD 372.652
```

Índice para catálogo sistemático:
1. Língua inglesa : Ensino fundamental   372.652

Aline Graziele Benitez – Bibliotecária – CRB-1/3129

All rights reserved.

MACMILLAN EDUCATION BRASIL
Av. Brigadeiro Faria Lima, 1.309, 2º Andar
Jd. Paulistano – São Paulo – SP – 01452-002
www.macmillan.com.br
Customer Service: [55] (11) 4613-2278
0800 16 88 77

Printed in Brazil. First print. August, 2023.

Gráfica Eskenazi

NOTES

NOTES